GREAT LIVES O[

JOHN BROWN

Edited by RICHARD WARCH
and JONATHAN F. FANTON

But thus saith the Lord,
Even the captives of the mighty shall be taken away,
and the prey of the terrible shall be delivered;
for I will contend with him that contendeth with thee,
and I will save thy children.
And I will feed them that oppress thee with their own flesh;
and they shall be drunken with their own blood,
as with sweet wine. . . .

—ISAIAH 49:25–26

For among my people are found wicked men:
they lay wait, as he that setteth snares;
they set a trap, they catch men.
Shall I not visit for these things? saith the Lord:
shall not my soul be avenged on such a nation as this?

—JEREMIAH 5:26,29

(Marked passages in John Brown's Bible)

A SPECTRUM BOOK

PRENTICE-HALL, INC., ENGLEWOOD CLIFFS, N.J.

Library of Congress Cataloging in Publication Data

WARCH, RICHARD, comp.
John Brown.

(Great lives observed) (A Spectrum Book)
Bibliography: p.
1. Brown, John, 1800–1859. 2. Harpers Ferry,
W. Va.—John Brown Raid, 1859—Sources. I. Fanton,
Jonathan F., joint comp. II. Title.
E451.W27   973.6′8′0924 [B]   73–2620
ISBN 0–13–510164–6
ISBN 0–13–510156–5 (pbk)

To the Students of History 22, 1970–1972

© 1973 by PRENTICE-HALL, INC.
Englewood Cliffs, New Jersey

A SPECTRUM BOOK

10 9 8 7 6 5 4 3 2 1

Printed in the United States of America

PRENTICE-HALL INTERNATIONAL, INC. (*London*)
PRENTICE-HALL OF AUSTRALIA, PTY. LTD. (*Sydney*)
PRENTICE-HALL OF CANADA, LTD. (*Toronto*)
PRENTICE-HALL OF INDIA PRIVATE LIMITED (*New Delhi*)
PRENTICE-HALL OF JAPAN, INC. (*Tokyo*)

Contents

PART ONE

JOHN BROWN AND THE HARPER'S FERRY RAID

1

2

3

4

Preparations and Pronouncements 41

The Account of the Chatham Convention by Dr. Martin R. Delany, *41* Portions of John Cook's "Confession," November, 1859, *43* "A Declaration of Liberty by the Representatives of the Slave Population of the United States of America," *46*

5

Postponement and Diversion 49

T. W. Higginson to Brown, May 7, 1858, *49* F. B. Sanborn to T. W. Higginson, May 11, 1858, *50* Portion of a Letter from Hugh Forbes to Dr. Samuel G. Howe, May 14, 1858, *50* Brown to F. B. Sanborn, May 14, 1858, *51* Gerrit Smith to F. B. Sanborn, July 26, 1858, *52*

6

Versions of the Plan 53

Richard J. Hinton's Interview with John Brown and John Kagi, *53* Frederick Douglass's Account of His Last Meeting with John Brown, August 19–21, 1859, *56*

7

The War Begins 59

F. B. Sanborn to T. W. Higginson, June 4, 1859, *60* J. H. Kagi to John Brown, Jr., October 10, 1859, *60* A Portion of John Cook's "Confession," November, 1859, *61* John E. P. Daingerfield's Account of the Raid, *62* Statements by Brown during and Immediately after the Raid, *66*

8

"A Conversation with Brown" 68

13

Editorial Reactions   119

14

A Divisive Issue: Partisan Responses   127

PART THREE

JOHN BROWN IN HISTORY

15

16

Acknowledgments

This book originated in 1970 as a collection of documents prepared for use in weekly discussion sections of the introductory American history course at Yale University. The collection was revised in 1971 and employed again in the course. Many people have assisted us during these past few years in assembling and teaching the several reincarnations of John Brown. Emmet McLaughlin, Robert Martin, Linda Warch, and especially Mary Noel helped at various stages in putting the documents and book together. Emmett Curran, Paul Czuchlewski, Carol O'Connor, Florence Peterson Dick, and Cathy Ross, instructors in History 22, all provided critiques of the documents. Our special thanks to Hal Williams, whose consent and encouragement made this endeavor possible, and to Margot Warch who, surprisingly enough, not only survived *John Brown* but helped him come into being.

Introduction

Observers of pre-Civil War America were uniformly impressed by the restless activity of its citizens. "It is strange to see with what feverish ardour the Americans pursue their own welfare," wrote the French observer Alexis de Tocqueville in the 1830s, "and to watch the vague dread that constantly torments them lest they should not have chosen the shortest path which may lead to it." In 1857, another European commentator, Adam de Gurowski, penned a similar observation: "Action carries them away, and they change with wonderful facility spots, abodes, regions, and states. . . . Mobility urges the American incessantly to work, to undertake, to spread, create, produce." Failure, Gurowski noted, was an anathema: "A man, in America, is not despised for being poor at the outset . . . but every year which passes, without adding to his prosperity, is a reproach to his understanding or industry."

Although these observations were meant to describe the character of Americans in general, they might also have been applied to John Brown in particular. For fifty-five of his fifty-nine years, John Brown was a man on the make who never made it. Few Americans pursued their own welfare with more feverish ardor than he, and few contemporaries changed states and occupations with more facility, or felt more reproached for being poor. Indeed, to examine John Brown's career before 1855 is not to observe a great life, but an average, even mediocre one.

John Brown, the second son of Owen and Ruth Brown, was born on May 9, 1800, in Torrington, Connecticut. Five years later Owen moved the family to the town of Hudson, in Ohio's Western Reserve, where he opened a tannery. Here John grew up, imbibing his father's Calvinist faith, strict discipline, and hatred of slavery. In 1816, hoping for a career in the Congregationalist ministry, John traveled to Plainfield, Massachusetts, to enroll in school, transferring after a few months to an academy in Litchfield, Connecticut. Although not a brilliant student, he worked faithfully at his studies and was disappointed when an inflammation of the eyes and a lack of funds forced him to abandon his education and return to Hudson.

For a time, John worked at his father's tannery, but he felt stifled in this subordinate role and, with his adopted brother, set up his own tannery on the outskirts of town. Determination and hard work paid off, and the new business flourished. As friends and acquaintances would later recall, the characteristics that would mark Brown's personality in later life were already apparent at this time. He was a young man who undertook no task or held no opinion halfheartedly. People were struck by his imperious demeanor and fervent faith. Brown possessed strong religious convictions, believing in a righteous and wrathful God, holding to the doctrines of human depravity and divine sovereignty, and trusting in God's providential direction of his life. He searched the Bible for God's will and discovered there, among other things, that to oppose slavery was to obey the Lord. Brown set about conveying this message to all he met and let it be known that he was prepared to act in accordance with that commandment. By the age of twenty he had already helped at least one fugitive slave escape to Canada.

But business and personal concerns, not antislavery activity, dominated Brown's early manhood. On June 21, 1820, he married Dianthe Lusk of Hudson; thirteen months later she gave birth to their first child, christened John Jr. In 1825, Brown made the first of what were to be many moves in his search for new and better opportunities. Motivated in part by the hope that a change of residence might improve his wife's health (she suffered from fits of mental despondency) and in part by simple restlessness, Brown moved his family to Randolph, Pennsylvania. There he bought 200 acres, cleared twenty-five, built a cabin and barn, and erected an eighteen-vat tannery. By the fall of 1826 the tannery was thriving, employing up to fifteen men; Brown also took up cattle-raising and commenced a six-year period of relative contentment and prosperity. He surveyed the community's roads, established a post office, opened a school, and exhorted his neighbors on matters of theology and discipline. Then adversity struck.

First, in March of 1831, his four-year-old son died. Soon afterward, Brown himself fell ill—probably with ague, a malarial-type fever which was to plague him throughout life—and his business began to sour. By 1832, he was in debt to friends and the bank; in the summer, Dianthe became sick. She died on August 10, shortly after the death of a new born son. She had given Brown seven children, five of whom survived childhood. Less than a year later, Brown remarried, taking as his wife Mary Ann Day, a stolid girl of sixteen. But financial troubles persisted; Brown was unable to collect money owed him and unable to pay what he owed others. In 1835, borrowing money for the move, he returned to Ohio in the hope of establishing a tanning industry with a wealthy partner.

Before the year was out, Brown's partner reneged on the tannery arrangement and John was out of work. But he was, if nothing else, quick to undertake new projects. This time it was land speculation. Brown plunged into this get-rich-quick scheme with more zeal than competence, and by the Panic of 1837 was hopelessly overextended. Creditors harassed him in the courts and once had him jailed, even though his misfortune was a product of ignorance rather than wrongdoing. Brown, acknowledging that his only error was doing business on credit, blamed his failure on the betrayal of so-called friends. He never recovered financially from this debacle, and spent the rest of his life in debt.

Brown's response to his latest disaster was typical—he tried something else. For a while he returned to tanning, then buying and selling cattle, next breeding racehorses, and finally tending sheep. Nothing worked. In September, 1842, he filed for bankruptcy. A year later, tragedy befell his family again when four children died of dysentery. Although Brown stated years later that during this period he had "a steady, strong desire to die," his resiliency prevailed. Despite his many trials and failures, he retained a reputation as a hard worker and a man of good and honest intentions. In 1844, trading in on this reputation, he entered a wool business partnership with Simon Perkins, a wealthy businessman from Akron. Typically, Brown threw himself into this venture with the passion of a convert and within two years had become convinced that wool growers were being fleeced by wool buyers. This conviction gave birth to a scheme, which he proposed to Perkins in 1846, to set up an office in Springfield, Massachusetts, with himself as manager to receive, sort, grade, and sell wool at fair prices. Perkins agreed to the idea and by June Brown was at work in Springfield. He labored long hours, but business conditions were unfavorable and, coupled with his poor bookkeeping and faulty pricing methods, soon had the company floundering. Although he rationalized to his customers "that some of the principal manufacturers are leagued together to break us down," some of the men who worked with him had a different explanation. One wool dealer, Aaron Erickson, later recalled that Brown had "almost a childlike ignorance of the great enterprise in which he was embarking" and would tolerate no criticism.

When Brown "claimed infallible accuracy in his discrimination," Erickson concluded that he was "a victim of his own delusions." John Brown was industrious and sincere, but he was no merchant.

The frustration of repeated failure in his drive for success, his prolonged absence from home, and the treadmill nature of his life took their toll on Brown. His letters to his family reveal his despair. He often apologized to his wife for the "poverty, trials, discredit and sore afflictions" with which he had burdened her, and thanked her for her constancy in the face of "all the follies and faults with which I am justly chargeable." Other letters found him wallowing in "very tedious business," having "considerable trouble in getting along," feeling "lonely and restless," and suffering "a great deal of anxiety about all at home." In moments of distress, Brown morbidly pondered his lot: "I feel considerable regret," he wrote Mary in 1847, "by turns that I have lived so many years, and have in reality done so little to increase the amount of human happiness. I often regret that my manner is no more kind and affectionate to those I really love and esteem; but I trust my friends will overlook my harsh, rough ways, when I cease to be in their way as an occasion of pain and unhappiness."

But his despondency was countered by his irrepressible optimism. Even when his fortunes were at their lowest ebb, Brown urged himself and his family on: "Let us try to maintain a cheerful self command while we are tossing up & down," he wrote, "& let our motto still be Action, Action." He was further sustained by his faith in God's purpose for his life and trusted that direction and success would be granted to him and his family. He hoped that the Browns would all "be disposed to acquiesce in the will of Providence. . . . He knows what is best, and may His holy will be done."

Still, business got no better. In 1849, Brown, ever resourceful when it came to money-making *ideas*, convinced Perkins and other wool growers to send him to England to sell their wool at decent prices. Before departing, however, Brown moved his family from Akron, where they had remained during his years in Springfield, to North Elba, New York. There they settled on lands that Gerrit Smith, the wealthy reformer-philanthropist, had set aside for Negro families. Brown had heard of Smith some years before when he had surveyed and made plans to settle on lands in Virginia which Smith had given to Oberlin College. The earlier plan never materialized, but the North Elba experiment intrigued Brown, who thought he could "be a kind of father" to the blacks there. After seeing that his family was settled in, Brown left for England in August. Two months later he was back, his hopes of reaping profits shattered.

In fact, Brown had lost about $40,000 on his scheme and once more faced the wrath and lawsuits of growers, creditors, and customers. Although he blamed his failure on the fact that he had "a great deal of stupid, obstinate prejudice to contend with, as well as conflicting interests," he still looked for victory in the defeat. "However much I may be blamed for doing poorly with the wool," he wrote Perkins, "I believe the wool business in the [United States] will be permanently helped by the means."

Despite the debacle, Perkins stuck by Brown. The two men agreed to close the Springfield depot in 1850, and the next year Brown returned to Ohio. He remained there for the next three years, traveling intermittently in futile attempts to recoup some of his losses. Again, financial woes were accompanied by family tragedy. His son Frederick, suffering from a mental derangement, grew worse; Brown fell victim to the ague; and a baby boy died of the whooping cough, his ninth child to be lost. Throughout this period Brown seemed beaten by his repeated reverses—he had suffered a total of fifteen business failures by this time—and unsure of his next move.

In 1854, after dissolving the relationship with Perkins, Brown made plans to return to North Elba. A little more than a year later he was on his way to Kansas, where he would quickly become caught up in the fervor of the pro- and antislavery agitation in the territory and within eight months would supervise the murders of five proslavery settlers. Here he would find his new calling and begin a second career. He did not know it at the time, but the consequences of that decision would raise him out of the obscurity that had shrouded his fifty-five years. Henceforth he would do battle with the enemies of God and dedicate his life to the eradication of slavery.

Although Brown's new life was in many ways to be a sharp departure from his past business career, it would also represent an intensification and fulfillment of long-held beliefs. Even though in his last years Brown was to condemn abolitionists as being "all talk and no action," he had from childhood been in accord with their position. His father had taught him to respect blacks and hate slavery, and the climate in which he had matured was rife with antislavery activity. Centered initially at Lane Seminary in Cincinnati and led by the revivalist Theodore Dwight Weld, antislavery sentiment soon spread to all parts of Ohio as the young Lane converts preached the message that Christianity and abolitionism were necessarily conjoined. Although many people objected to the abolitionist impulse, this gospel was one in which John Brown fervently believed: God commanded that slavery be destroyed. Brown was visibly shocked by the murder of the abolitionist editor Elijah Lovejoy at Alton, Illinois, in 1837 and, at a public meeting held in Hudson on the occasion, rose to proclaim that he would consecrate his life to the overthrow of slavery.

His record in acting on his convictions, however, was a spotty one. His one consistent practice was to assist runaway slaves—an activity he undertook with passion—but he never joined an antislavery society or participated in formal abolitionist groups. The first written evidence of his interest in assisting blacks in an organized fashion appeared in a letter of November 20, 1834, to his brother Frederick. Brown wrote that he hoped to adopt a Negro boy and also confessed that he had "for years been trying to devise some way to get a school a-going" for blacks in Randolph, Pennsylvania. The education of young blacks, he thought, might "do more toward breaking their yoke effectually" than any other means. But nothing came of either plan and though he continued to manifest an interest in the slavery issue and persisted in aiding fugitive slaves, he was essentially inactive in this endeavor until the late 1840s.

Brown's antislavery sentiments became more militant during his stay in Springfield, Massachusetts. There he read the works of extreme abolitionists of the William Lloyd Garrison school (although he had first read *The Liberator* in the 1830s), and got to know a number of blacks, both freedmen and runaways. He also met several prominent Negroes, including James W. Loguen and the radical Henry Highland Garnet in New York and Frederick Douglass in Springfield. These contacts evidently spurred Brown on to a flurry of activity. In late 1847 or early 1848 he wrote an article entitled "Sambo's Mistakes" for the Negro newspaper *The Ram's Horn,* in which he posed as a black taking his fellows to task for their errors. Brown admonished his readers about personal habits of thought and behavior and concluded the piece with a thinly veiled invitation to blacks to cast off their submissive status in favor of an independent one. "Another trifling error of my life," he confessed, "has been that I have always expected to secure the favour of the whites by tamely submitting to every species of indignity contempt & wrong instead of nobly resisting their brutal aggressions from principle & taking my place as a man & assuming the responsibilities of a man."

Brown not only counseled blacks to resist aggression, but was prepared to do so himself. In November, 1847, he met Frederick Douglass and proposed a scheme for engaging in guerrilla activity in the South as a means of running off slaves. This so-called "Subterranean Pass Way" plan—Brown's action-oriented version of the Underground Railroad—was to remain a germ in his mind in the years ahead, but in the late 1840s it never progressed past the stage of speculation. Instead, he hit upon the idea of moving his family to Gerrit Smith's land in upstate New York, where he could assist the free blacks who had settled there. In 1851, back in Springfield after his abortive trip abroad, Brown again became involved in the antislavery cause by forming an organization of blacks to resist anyone who attempted to enforce the Fugitive Slave Law. The League of Gileadites, as it was called, was a militant group in which secrecy, resolution, and violence were to be practiced. *"Let the first blow be the signal for all to engage,"* Brown advised the members, *"and when engaged do not do your work by halves, but make clean work with your enemies."*

For Brown, the Fugitive Slave Law was only one example of the ways in which the national government sanctioned the evil institution of slavery. In the early 1850s his contempt for the government—and, by extension, for all legal remedies to the slavery issue—grew sharper. On January 9, 1854, in a letter to Frederick Douglass, Brown gave vent to his feelings in reference to the Kansas-Nebraska debate in Congress: "What, I ask, could possibly tend so to destroy all possible respect for legislators, president, judges, or other magistrates or officers—or to root out all confidence in the integrity of civil rulers and courts, as well as legislative bodies, as the passing of enactments which it is self-evident are most abominably wicked and unjust, dignifying them with the name of laws, and then employing the public purse and sword to execute them?"

By the early 1850s, then, John Brown's concern for the plight of blacks, his hatred of the institution of slavery, and his despair over the nation's capacity to deal effectively with either had intensified and found expression in increasingly violent schemes and exhortations. It also seems evident that during this period of his life—one marked by frustration and frenetic behavior—Brown was searching for ways to fulfill his dream of increasing "the amount of human happiness" and of serving his God. Indeed, the desire to serve the Lord was a principal motivation throughout Brown's life, and he constantly searched for the signs which would reveal God's purpose for him. His sons' decision to go to Kansas in 1854, as it turned out, provided him with the occasion to hear and heed those signs.

John Jr., Jason, Owen, Salmon, and Frederick left Ohio for Kansas both in search of a new start in farming and in response to the call for men to join the free-state settlers who were fighting for supremacy in that embattled territory. At first, Brown declined to go along, stating that he felt committed to work at North Elba. Then he wavered, and sought advice from friends and family. In a letter to his daughter Ruth he proposed the thesis that to move to Kansas would be "more likely to benefit the colored people *on the whole* than to return with them to N. Elba," but asked that she solicit the opinions of "all the colored people" of that community: "As I volunteered in their service; (or the service of the colored people); they have a right to vote, as to [the] course I take." He also asked Gerrit Smith and Frederick Douglass for their counsel.

Smith, at least, wanted Brown to return to North Elba, and although he took his family there in June, 1855, he was in the process of succumbing to his sons' pleas to join them in Kansas. Their letters told of the proslavery depradations in the territory and conveyed a sense of purpose and excitement. "If the question of Slavery or no Slavery in Kansas must be settled at the cartridge box, instead of at the ballot box," John Jr. wrote his father, "I pray the day may speedily come. Every day strengthens my belief that the sword, that final arbiter of all the great questions that have stirred mankind, will soon be called on to give its verdict." Salmon echoed the same aggressiveness: "I feel more like fight now than I ever did before, and would be glad to go to Alabama. I have no doubt of the success of the plan."

These sentiments were enough for Brown and he determined to go to Kansas. Although no evidence survives about an Alabama plan, perhaps Brown had speculated about putting his Subterranean Pass Way into operation in the deep South. In any case, before leaving, he traveled throughout the East collecting guns and ammunition from sympathetic committees which had been established to assist the free-state settlers. By the time he left for Kansas in August he was armed for battle.

Kansas in the mid-1850s was the ideal location for Brown to undertake his new mission. There northerners and southerners, antislavery and proslavery advocates, and—in Brown's eyes—the forces of good and evil met face to face. Following the 1854 passage of the Kansas-Nebraska Act, which provided that the people of the territory were to vote on the existence of slavery there (Senator Stephen Douglas's "popular soverignty" solution to the salvery extension crisis), both the North and the South attempted to pack Kansas with sympathetic settlers. The immediate result was conflict and bloodshed, with proslavery men entering the territory from Missouri to harass free-state men and stuff the ballot box with proslavery votes. For the next several years the competing forces would continue to elect their own officials and write their own constitutions and the "Kansas Question" would remain in the forefront of national affairs. The chaos of the situation there caused embarrassment and division in Washington and, in fact, split the Democratic Party and helped create the Republican Party. These larger events, with which John Brown had little to do, formed the background for his activities in 1856.

From the moment he entered the territory, Brown evidently relished its warlike atmosphere and itched to get into a fight. "For one," he wrote Mary in April, 1856, "I have no desire (all things considered) to have the slave-power cease from its acts of aggression. 'Their foot shall slide in due time.' " On May 21–22, almost as a fulfillment of Brown's wish, a force of proslavery agitators sacked the free-state town of Lawrence, burning buildings, destroying newspaper presses, and killing two men. On the night of May 24, Brown struck a blow of reprisal. With four sons, a son-in-law, and two others, he entered the Pottawatomie settlement and brutally murdered five proslavery men. Though Brown apparently killed no one himself, he was responsible for directing the attack. "God is my judge," Brown reputedly told his son Jason, "we were justified under the circumstances."

Justified or not, Brown's actions intensified an already charged atmosphere. It has been estimated that between November, 1855, and December, 1856, about 200 men were killed and around two million dollars' worth of property destroyed in the territory. The Brown family, led by the old man, was in the thick of the battle. He went into hiding after the Pottawatomie killings and two of his sons—neither of whom had participated in the affair—were arrested. Although later released, both John Jr. and Jason were maligned and mistreated during their confinement, an experience that left John Jr. practically deranged. On June 2, Brown attacked and conquered a band of Missourians led by Captain Henry Pate (a deputy U.S. marshal), which had entered Kansas to round up Brown and others. Brown's victory over numerically superior forces at the battle of Black Jack bolstered his reputation as a fighter and gave him confidence in his mission. That mission, he fervently believed, was commissioned by the Lord: "God," he wrote, "who has not given us over to the will of our enemies, but has moreover delivered them into our hand, will, we humbly trust, still keep and deliver us."

The success at Black Jack was followed by other engagements. In August he and several dozen followers fought off and eventually escaped from a force of over 200 proslavery attackers at Osawatomie, Brown's home base. His son Frederick was killed in this battle and the Osawatomie settlement burned. This experience, coupled with his earlier adventures in the territory, nurtured in Brown an abiding conviction. As he surveyed the ruins, Brown supposedly vowed that he would "die fighting for this cause" and predicted that "there will be no more peace in this land until slavery is done for. I will give them something else to do than to extend slave territory. I will carry this war into Africa." As events were to prove, this was no idle threat.

In the fall of 1856, Brown went into hiding and engaged in other guerrilla skirmishes against proslavery groups, but under the firm leadership of territorial governor John W. Geary, Kansas gradually quieted down. For Brown, however, the lull in the action did not mean that the battle was over. In November he left for the East in order to solicit funds to continue the fight. He arrived in Boston shortly after the new year, 1857.

He went first to see Franklin B. Sanborn, secretary of the Massachusetts State Kansas Committee, and presented several letters of introduction. Sanborn, taken by Brown's "singular blending of the soldier and the deacon" and impressed by his commitment to the antislavery crusade, agreed to help collect funds for the old man's activities in Kansas. He introduced Brown to a number of sympathetic men (among them William Lloyd Garrison), particularly Thomas Wentworth Higginson, a minister in Worcester, Theodore Parker, the radical Unitarian preacher, Dr. Samuel Gridley Howe, a well-known humanitarian, and George Luther Stearns, a wealthy manufacturer and chairman of the Massachusetts Committee. With the support of these five men, the Massachusetts Committee voted on January 7 to make Brown its agent and gave him 200 Sharpe's rifles and several boxes of ammunition which it had stored at Tabor, Iowa. Several weeks later, at the prompting of his Massachusetts friends, the National Kansas Committee voted to donate supplies and money to Brown's cause, a pledge later canceled for lack of funds.

For the next few months, Brown continued his fund-raising campaign, speaking to groups in Worcester, Springfield, New Haven, New York, Syracuse, and Boston (where he met Henry David Thoreau and Ralph Waldo Emerson). He told his listeners about his trials and sufferings in Bleeding Kansas (without mentioning the Pottawatomie murders) and asked for support for his future work. On March 4 he published an appeal for "contributions of pecuniary aid" for his work from "all honest lovers of *Liberty* and *Human Rights*." On the whole, however, Brown was disappointed in these efforts; he received many pledges but little cash. Even Gerrit Smith turned down the old man's request; only industrialist Amos Lawrence, Sanborn, and Stearns came through with money.

In March, Brown was in New York City, where he met Hugh Forbes, an English soldier of fortune who had fought with Garibaldi in Italy in 1848 and who fancied himself a military tactician. Forbes had been taken by abolitionism and the disunion movement and was intrigued by Brown's aggressive plans for guerrilla warfare in the South. Brown was equally enthused by Forbes and hired him to be the drillmaster for his men and to write them a handbook of tactics. The two men agreed to meet in Tabor, Iowa, in the summer. Brown, using the alias Nelson Hawkins, traveled back and forth in the Northeast for the next few months and in mid-May set out for Iowa. He stopped to visit with family in Hudson, Ohio, for a while and on August 7 arrived in Tabor. The climactic stage of his career was about to begin.

It is at this point in the life of John Brown that the documents in the volume commence. Following two introductory sections on Brown's autobiographical recollections of his first thirty years and several accounts of his Kansas experiences of 1856, the documents continue the narrative of his career as he began the intense and at times confusing preparation for his war against the Slave Power. This book is about those final years. In preparing this collection, the editors have focused the primary evidence in Parts One and Two on the one event with which John Brown is uniquely connected—the raid on Harper's Ferry, Virginia, in October, 1859.[1] Indeed, Brown's right to be included in the *Great Lives Observed* series is based solely on this singular moment. Without it, John Brown would not merit our attention. Because of it, he captured the attention of his generation, has been memorialized in song and legend, and has fascinated Americans ever since.

The documents that follow are designed to reveal both John Brown the man and Harper's Ferry as plan and event. Specifically, the materials present information about (1) the maturation of Brown's intentions and plans in the period before Harper's Ferry; (2) what others knew of those intentions; (3) the raid itself; (4) the development of Brown's character during these crucial years; and (5) the evolution of John Brown as a symbolic figure in the post-raid months. In effect, then, this book covers a little more than two years in the life of its subject. Although the period is brief, Brown spent this time in ardent thought and feverish activity. Character traits and ideological beliefs he had long possessed appear in bold relief in these final, frantic years. In reading his private letters and semipublic writings, one comes to discover John Brown in all his complexity and ambiguity.

This book has been constructed as an exercise in inquiry and discovery. Its purpose is to unfold the drama of John Brown, Harper's Ferry, and the responses to both through a collection of primary evidence. The editors have not attempted to program this material toward specific conclusions about Brown; much of it is contradictory and inconclusive. Only by piecing it all together will the reader be able to make his own judgments about who John Brown was and what he meant to the Americans of his day. Part Three provides the reader with the opportunity to test his own assessments against those of seven historians, as well as the chance to compare the various historians with each other.

The following pages, then, are not only about a man but also about the event that gave his life meaning. The remainder of the Introduction will trace Brown's movements leading up to that event, leaving to the documents the task of revealing the particularities of how Brown's plan evolved, took place, and was received.

[1] In 1859, what is now Harpers Ferry, West Virginia, was Harper's Ferry, Virginia.

On August 9, Hugh Forbes joined Brown in Tabor. Within weeks the two men were quarreling about plans and tactics, finally compromising on what Forbes was to call the "Well-Matured Plan" for combating slavery in the South. But the truce was an uneasy one. The old man was obviously planning something, but he told his recruits and backers only that it was *"secret service & no questions asked."* For the next few months Forbes impatiently awaited the arrival of both his troops and his pay, but no money was forthcoming, and by November, when the group departed for Kansas, Forbes was considerably disgruntled. Before the party reached the territory he left and returned East.

Brown found Kansas relatively quiet in the aftermath of the free-state victory in the October elections and so returned with his men—who by this time numbered ten—to Iowa. There he told his young followers that their mission was "troubling Israel" by an incursion into Virginia to run off slaves. Although many of them had supposed they were to serve in Kansas, the old man's indomitable conviction of the rightness of his scheme convinced them to go along. In January, 1858, Brown left his men in Springdale, Iowa, and set off for Frederick Douglass's home in Rochester, New York.

There he discussed his plans with the Negro leader and gave more thought to Forbes's criticism that his attempt at a slave insurrection might collapse into complete chaos. To meet this objection Brown wrote a Provisional Constitution that would create the government for a new state in the region of his invasion. Brown's purpose in life was at last set—he would be God's avenger against the forces of evil. If anything "explains" John Brown it is this singular conviction. His letters and writings from his years in Kansas to his death abound with it. In January, 1858, he wrote his wife that he was hopeful that "the great work of my life (the unseen Hand that 'guided me, and who has indeed holden my right hand, may hold it still,' though I have not known him at all as I ought) I may yet see accomplished (God helping) and be permitted to return and 'rest at evening.' "

In the next few months he met with his eastern sympathizers, first with Sanborn at Gerrit Smith's house in Peterboro, New York, and later with Higginson, Parker, Stearns, Howe, and Sanborn in Boston. Although it is not clear how much detailed information Brown conveyed at these gatherings, he did indicate that he intended a foray into the South to free slaves. The several men consented to such a scheme and in March formed themselves into a secret Committee of Six (the five Massachusetts men plus Smith) to assist Brown in his plan, mainly by raising money.

Brown continued to keep in touch with the Secret Six, alternately asking them for funds and telling them about his "mission," but his letters to them and others offered few clues as to what he actually intended to do. All they revealed was that Brown proposed to go to "Africa" or "China" (the South), equipped with "furniture," "tools" or "hardware" (weapons), accompanied by "scholars," "shepherds" or "reapers" (recruits), in order to set up a "school," undertake "prospecting," speculate "in wool," do "Kansas work," or engage in the "railroad business on a somewhat extended scale." It all sounded very conspiratorial and exciting.

In the spring of 1858 Brown's spirits were high. After his meeting with Sanborn and Smith he wrote the former that his plan constituted his "one opportunity" in life to engage in service to a cause with "mighty and soul-satisfying rewards." He expected to "effect a mighty conquest, even though," he ominously warned, "it be like the last victory of Samson." He expressed the same exuberance in a letter to Ohio Congressman Joshua Giddings: "The slave will be delivered by the shedding of blood, and the signs are multiplying that his deliverance is at hand."

It was in this mood of impending action that Brown left for Chatham, Canada, in May. There he convened a convention to formulate plans for a government he intended to establish in the areas he conquered. With the assistance of Dr. Martin R. Delany, a prominent Negro leader, Brown assembled thirty-four blacks and twelve whites to hear and adopt his paramilitary Provisional Constitution. Fittingly and expectedly, the convention elected John Brown Commander-in-Chief and named his friend John Henrie Kagi Secretary of War, leaving the office of President of the Provisional Republic vacant. Though Brown's men discussed his plan in private sessions at Chatham, it is doubtful that others who attended the convention knew of the scheme for a southern invasion.

But just as it appeared that Brown was ready to act, the plan began to come unstuck. Hugh Forbes, the drillmaster who had been pestering Brown's supporters for money and dropping damaging hints to various U.S. Senators since mid-winter, wrote Howe in May threatening to expose the plot. Howe and Higginson wanted Brown to go ahead anyway, but the other backers counseled postponement. Stearns went so far as to order Brown not to use the weapons given him for his Kansas work anywhere else. After much consultation it was agreed that Brown should return to Kansas until the next spring in order to throw Forbes off the scent and cast doubt on the validity of his disclosures. Brown reluctantly agreed and in June, under the name Shubel Morgan, he left for the West.

For the next six months he remained in and around Kansas, where he joined forces with James Montgomery, who was leading free-state settlers in raids into Missouri. But Montgomery proved too timid for Brown, and on December 20 the old warrior conducted his own raid into the neighboring state, liberating eleven slaves and making off with horses, wagons, property, and two white prisoners. Although he was roundly criticized for his daring act by Kansans who desired peace and feared reprisals, Brown defended his "work" against all objections. On January 20, 1859, he left the territory with the ex-slaves and, eluding posses along the way, guided them to Detroit and placed them on a ferry for Canada.

For the next few months Brown traveled through Ohio, New York, Connecticut, and Massachusetts rounding up support for his mission. On May 9 he delivered an impassioned lecture in Concord. Bronson Alcott, who attended along with Emerson and Thoreau, noted that Brown had been vague about his destination but left no doubt about "his readiness to strike a blow for freedom at the proper moment." Alcott thought Brown "equal to anything he dares—the man to do the deed, if it must be done, and with the martyr's temper and purpose. . . . I think him about the manliest man I have ever seen—the type and synonym of the Just."

On June 3 he was in Collinsville, Connecticut, where he contracted with Charles Blair to finish the thousand pikes he had ordered from him two years earlier. He paid a final visit to his family in North Elba, arranged for the guns and ammunition stored in Ohio to be shipped to Chambersburg, Pennsylvania, and in late June set out for Virginia. On July 3 he was in Harper's Ferry. A few days later, calling himself Isaac Smith, he rented the Kennedy farmhouse in nearby Maryland. There he awaited the arrival of his recruits and finalized his plans. But the recruits never arrived— at least not in the numbers Brown expected—and some of those who were there grew restless. Only when Brown threatened to resign as commander did they rally back to his side. At last Brown decided he was ready. At eight o'clock on the night of Sunday, October 16, Brown set out with eighteen of his men—leaving three behind as a rear guard—to begin his war against slavery.

The "war" lasted less than two days. Though initial reports of the raid exaggerated its dimensions, by Monday it became clear that there were only a handful of invaders. On Tuesday morning, October 18, U.S. Marines under the command of Colonel Robert E. Lee stormed the engine house, where the remnants of Brown's band had taken refuge, and killed or captured the raiders. Of the twenty-one men who had accompanied Brown, five escaped (including his son Owen), ten were killed (including his sons Watson and Oliver), and six were captured along with their leader. On October 25, still suffering from wounds inflicted by his captors, John Brown was brought to trial by the state of Virginia in Charlestown. Six days later he was convicted on all three counts: conspiring with slaves to rebel, murder, and treason. On December 2 he was hung in Charlestown. "So perish all enemies of Virginia!" intoned an officer at his death, "All such enemies of the Union! All such foes of the human race!"

This judgment no doubt represented the opinion of Virginians, but the verdict was a sectional one. Southerners, fearing that there might be other John Browns and other raids, reacted to Harper's Ferry with an hysteria which often resulted in the enactment of repressive laws, the implementation of censorship, and the creation of vigilance committees. While many northerners disowned Brown and deplored his violent act, others, inspired by Brown's courage and rectitude, paid tribute to him and his bold attempt. Indeed, in the months after his capture, John Brown and the Harper's Ferry raid became the subjects of intense controversy. Ministers, politicians, editors, and everyday citizens confronted and sought to interpret the man and the event. They were ably assisted in this task by John Brown himself, who spent the six weeks in jail before his execution writing letters of explanation and justification to family, friends, and correspondents. By the time of his death, he was already a symbolic figure, standing for good or evil, purposefulness or madness, depending on the views of the beholder.

John Brown and the Harper's Ferry raid further polarized an already divided nation and served as a grim foreboding that the resolution of that division would be violent and bloody. It was somehow fitting that as the northern armies advanced into the South during the Civil War, John Brown's soul went "marching on" with them.

Richard Warch

Chronology of the Life of John Brown

1800	(May 9) Born in Torrington, Connecticut.
1805	Family migrates to Ohio.
1816–17	Attends schools in Massachusetts and Connecticut.
1819–25	Works as a tanner in Hudson, Ohio.
1820	(June 21) Marries Dianthe Lusk.
1825–35	Works as a tanner in Randolph, Pa., and is postmaster.
1832	(August 10) Dianthe dies after giving birth to their seventh child.
1833	(July 11) Marries Mary Ann Day.
1835–40	Lives near Hudson, Ohio, and speculates in land.
1841	Begins sheep-farming.
1842	Declares bankruptcy.
1844–51	Joins with Simon Perkins in wool merchant partnership. Manages company warehouse in Springfield, Mass.
1847	Frederick Douglass visits Brown and learns of his plan to free slaves.
1847–48	Writes "Sambo's Mistakes" for The Ram's Horn.
1849	Moves family to North Elba, New York, and travels to Europe in effort to sell wool at better prices.
1851	Founds the League of Gileadites in Springfield and returns to Ohio with his family.
1855	Moves family back to North Elba. (June) Attends Syracuse convention of abolitionists. (October 6) Arrives in Kansas.
1856	(May 23–24) Pottawatomie murders. (June 2) Battle of Black Jack.
1857	(January–March) Tours in the East in search of funds. (March) Contracts with Charles Blair of Connecticut for 1,000 pikes. (August–November) At Tabor, Iowa, with Hugh Forbes to found military training school.
1858	(February) Visits with Frederick Douglass in Rochester, New York. (May 8–10) At Chatham, Ontario, Canada for convention that adopts the Provisional Constitution. (June) Returns to Kansas for diversionary activity after Forbes's disclosure of plans.

(December 20) Conducts a raid into Missouri, freeing eleven slaves.

1859 (January–February) Leads fugitives to Detroit and sends them to Canada.

(April–May) Returns East and pays last visit to North Elba.

(May–June) In Boston with members of the Secret Six.

(July 3) Arrives at Harper's Ferry.

(October 16) Raid begins.

(October 18) Captured at daybreak.

(October 25–November 4) Preliminary hearing and trial at Charlestown, Virginia. Sentenced to hang.

(December 2) Executed at Charlestown.

(December 8) Buried at North Elba.

PART ONE

JOHN BROWN AND THE HARPER'S FERRY RAID

Historians who have examined the primary evidence concerning John Brown and the Harper's Ferry raid have made various and contradictory judgments about both. Part One includes a representative sample of the important primary documents on which assessments of Brown have been based. Among those issues which have figured prominently in traditional assessments of Brown are: the substance, development, and tactical soundness of the Harper's Ferry plan; the character of Brown's supporters and their knowledge of his plan; Brown's prior expectations for the raid compared to his later explanations of his intentions; and finally, the question of Brown's self-image and mental stability. Although no one piece of evidence can answer any given question about Brown, the materials as a whole provide the raw data for sound—and competing—historical interpretations. Each individual who confronts the evidence about John Brown will, of course, have particular concerns and ask different questions.

1

An Autobiographical Letter

On July 15, 1857, Brown wrote a revealing letter to thirteen-year-old Harry Stearns, son of wealthy New England merchant George Luther Stearns, who was chairman of the Massachusetts Kansas Committee. Brown met Stearns in January, 1857, and from then on Stearns was one of his most generous financial backers. This letter was written, in part, to convince the elder Stearns of Brown's integrity and lifelong commitment to fight against slavery. The letter provides much

of what is known about Brown's early life, although it stops
short of the years of trial and failure between 1831 and 1856.[1]

I have not forgotten my promise to write you; but my constant
care, & anxiety have obliged me to put it off a long time. I do not
flatter myself that I *can* write anything which will very much interest you: but have concluded to send you a short story of a certain
boy of my acquaintance: & for convenience & shortness of name, I
will call him John. This story will be mainly a narration of follies
and errors; which it is to be hoped *you may avoid;* but there is one
thing connected with it, which will be calculated to encourage any
young person to persevering effort; & that is the degree of success *in*
accomplishing his objects which to a great degree marked the course
of this boy throughout my entire acquaintance with him; notwithstanding his moderate capacity; & still more moderate acquirements.

John was born May 9th, 1800, at Torrington, Litchfield Co.
Connecticut; of poor but respectable parents: a decendant on the
side of his father of one of the company of the Mayflower who
landed at Plymouth 1620. His mother was decended from a man
who came at an early period to New England from Amsterdam, in
Holland. Both his Father's and his Mother's Fathers served in the
war of the revolution: His Father's Father; died in a barn in New
York while in the service; in 1776.

I can not tell you of anything in the first Four years of John's life
worth mentioning save that at that *early age* he was tempted by
Three large Brass Pins belonging to a girl who lived in the family
& *stole them.* In this he was detected by his Mother; & after having
a full day to think of the wrong; received from her a thorough whip-
ping. When he was Five years old his Father moved to Ohio; then
a wilderness filled with wild beasts, & Indians. During the long journey, which was performed in part or mostly with an *ox-team;* he
was called on by turns to assist a boy Five years older (who had
been adopted by his Father & Mother) & learned to think he could
accomplish *smart things* in driving the Cows; & riding the horses.
Sometimes he met with Rattle Snakes which were very large; &
which some of the company generally managed to kill. After getting
to Ohio in 1805 he was for some time rather afraid of the Indians,
& of their Rifles; but this soon wore off: & he used to hang about

[1] From Franklin B. Sanborn, ed., *The Life and Letters of John Brown* (Boston:
Roberts Brothers, 1891), pp. 12–17. Footnotes have been omitted.

them quite as much as was consistent with good manners; & learned a trifle of their talk. His father learned to dress Deer Skins, & at 6 years old John was installed a young Buck Skin. He was perhaps rather observing as he ever after remembered the entire process of Deer Skin *dressing;* so that he could at any time dress his own leather such as Squirel, Raccoon, Cat, Wolf and Dog Skins, and also learned to make Whip Lashes, which brought him some change at times, & was of considerable service in many ways. At Six years old he began to be a rambler in the wild new country finding birds and squirrels and sometimes a wild Turkey's nest. But about this period he was placed in the school of *adversity;* which my young friend was a most necessary part of his early training. You may *laugh* when you come to read about it; but these were *sore trials* to John: whose earthly treasures were very *few* & *small.* These were the beginning of a severe but *much needed course* of discipline which he afterwards was to pass through; & which it is to be hoped has learned him before this time that the Heavenly Father sees it best to take all the little things out of his hands which he has ever placed in them. When John was in his Sixth year a poor *Indian boy* gave him a Yellow Marble the first he had ever seen. This he thought a great deal of; & kept it a good while; but at last *he lost it* beyond recovery. *It took years to heal the wound* & I *think* he cried at times about it. About Five months after this he caught a young Squirrel tearing off his tail in doing it; & getting severely bitten at the same time himself. He however held on *to the little bob tail Squirrel;* & finally got him perfectly tamed, so that he almost idolized his pet. *This too he lost;* by its wandering away; or by getting killed; & for a year or two John was *in mourning;* and looking at all the Squirrels he could see to try & discover Bobtail, *if possible.* I must not neglect to tell you of a verry *bad & foolish* habbit to which John was somewhat addicted. I mean *telling lies;* generally to screen himself from blame; or from punishment. He could not well endure to be reproached; & I now think had he been oftener encouraged to be entirely frank; *by making frankness a kind of atonement* for some of his faults; he would not have been so often guilty of this fault; nor have been (in after life) obliged to struggle *so long* with *so mean* a habit.

John was *never quarelsome;* but was *excessively* fond of the *hardest & roughest* kind of plays; & could *never get enough* [of] them. Indeed when for a short time he was sometimes sent to School the opportunity it afforded to wrestle & Snow ball & run & jump & knock off old seedy Wool hats; offered to him almost the only compensation for the confinement, & restraints of school. I need not tell you that with such a feeling & but little chance of going to school *at all:* he did not become much of a schollar. He would always choose to stay at home & work hard rather than be sent to school; & during the warm season might generally be seen *barefooted & bareheaded:* with Buck skin Breeches suspended often with one leather strap over his shoulder but sometimes with Two. To be sent off through the wilderness alone to very considerable distances was particularly his delight; & in this he was often indulged so that by the time he was Twelve years old he was sent off more than a Hundred Miles with companies of cattle; & he would have thought his character much injured had he been obliged to be helped in any such job. This was a boyish kind of feeling but characteristic however.

At Eight years old, John was left a Motherless boy which loss was complete & pearmanent for notwithstanding his Father again married to a sensible, intelligent, and on many accounts a very estimable woman; yet he never *adopted her in feeling;* but continued to pine after his own Mother for years. This opperated very unfavourably uppon him; as he was both naturally fond of females; &, withall, extremely diffident; & deprived him of a suitable connecting link between the different sexes; the want of which might under some circumstances, have proved his ruin.

When the war broke out *with England,* his Father soon commenced furnishing the troops with beef cattle, the collecting & driving of which afforded him some opportunity for the chase (on foot) of wild steers & other cattle through the woods. During this war he had some chance to form his own boyish judgment of *men & measures:* & to become somewhat familiarly acquainted with some who have figured before the country since that time. The effect of what he saw during the war was to so far disgust him with Military affairs that he would neither train, *or drill;* but paid fines; & got along like a Quaker until his age finally has cleared him of Military duty.

During the war with England a circumstance occurred that in the end made him a most *determined Abolitionist:* & led him to declare, *or Swear: Eternal war* with Slavery. He was staying for a short time with a very gentlemanly landlord since a United States Marshall who held a slave boy near his own age very active, inteligent and good feeling; & to whom John was under considerable obligation for numerous little acts of kindness. *The master* made a great pet of John: brought him to table with his first company; & friends; called their attention to every little smart thing he *said or did:* & to the fact of his being more than a hundred miles from home with a company of cattle alone; while the *negro boy* (who was fully if not more than his equal) was badly clothed, poorly fed; *& lodged in cold weather; &* beaten before his eyes with Iron Shovels or any other thing that came first to hand. This brought John to reflect on the wretched, hopeless condition, of *Fatherless* & *Motherless* slave *children:* for such children have neither Fathers or Mothers to protect, & provide for them. He sometimes would raise the question *is God their Father?*

At the age of Ten years an old friend induced him to read a little history, & offered him the free use of a good library; by; which he acquired some taste for reading: which formed the principle part of his early education: & diverted him in a great measure from bad company. He by this means grew to be verry fond of the company, & conversation of old & intelligent persons. He never attempted to dance in his life; nor did he ever learn to know *one* of a pack of *Cards* from *another.* He learned nothing of Grammer; nor did he get at school so much knowledge of common Arithmetic as the Four ground rules. This will give you some general idea of the first Fifteen years of his life; during which time he became very strong & large of his age & ambitious to perform the full labour of a man; at almost any kind of hard work. By reading the lives of great, wise & good men their sayings, and writings; he grew to a dislike of vain & frivolous *conversation & persons;* & was often greatly obliged by the kind manner in which older & more inteligent persons treated him at their houses: & in conversation; which was a great relief on account of his extreme bashfulness.

He very early in life became ambitious to excel in doing anything he undertook to perform. This kind of feeling I would recommend to all young persons both *male & female:* as it will certainly tend to secure admission to the company of the more intelligent; & better portion of every community. By all means endeavour to excel in some laudable pursuit.

I had like to have forgotten to tell you of one of John's misfortunes which set rather hard on him while a young boy. He had by some means *perhaps* by gift of his father become the owner of a little Ewe Lamb which did finely till it was about Two Thirds grown; & then sickened & died. This brought another protracted *mourning season:* not that he felt the pecuniary loss so much: for that was never his disposition; but so strong & earnest were his atachments.

John had been taught from earliest childhood to "fear God and keep his commandments;" & though quite skeptical he had always by turns felt much serious doubt as to his future well being; & about this time became to some extent a convert to Christianity & ever after a firm believer in the divine authenticity of the Bible. With this book he became very familiar, & possessed a most unusual memory of its entire contents.

Now some of the things I have been *telling of;* were just such as I would recommend to you: & I would like to know that you had selected these out; & adopted them as part of your own plan of life; & I wish you to have *some deffinite plan.* Many seem to have none; & others never stick to any that they do form. This was not the case with John. He followed up with *tenacity* whatever he set about so long as it answered his general purpose: & hence he rarely failed in some good degree to effect the things he undertook. This was so much the case that he *habitually expected to succeed* in his undertakings. With this feeling *should be coupled;* the consciousness that our plans are right in themselves.

During the period I have named, John had acquired a kind of ownership to certain animals of some little value but as he had come to understand that the *title of minors* might be a little imperfect: he had recourse to various means in order to secure a more *independent;* & perfect right of property. One of those means was to exchange with his Father for something of far less value. Another was by trading with others persons for something his Father had never owned. Older persons have some times found difficulty with *titles.*

From Fifteen to Twenty years old, he spent most of his time working at the Tanner & Currier's trade keeping Bachelors hall; & he officiating as Cook; & for most of the time as foreman of the establishment under his Father. During this period he found much trouble with some of the bad habits I have mentioned & with some that I have not told you off: his conscience urging him forward with great power in this matter: but his close attention to *business;* & success in its management; together with the way he got along with a company of men, & boys; made him quite a favorite with the serious & more inteligent portion of older persons. This was so much the case; & secured for him so many little notices from those he esteemed; that his vanity was very much fed by it: & he came forward to manhood quite full of self-conceit; & self-confident; notwithstanding his *extreme* bashfulness. A younger brother used sometimes to remind him of this: & to repeat to him *this expression* which you may somewhere find, "A King against whom there is no rising up." The habit so early formed of being obeyed rendered him in after life too much disposed to speak in an imperious or dictating way. From Fifteen years & upward he felt a good deal of anxiety to learn; but could only read & studdy a little; both for want of time; & on account of inflammation of the eyes. He however managed by the help of books to make himself tolerably well acquainted with common arithmetic; & Surveying; which he practiced more or less after he was Twenty years old.

At a little past Twenty years led by his own inclination & *prompted also* by his Father, he married a *remarkably plain;* but neat industrious & economical girl; of excellent character; earnest piety; & good practical common sense; about one year younger than himself. This woman by her mild, frank, & *more than all else:* by her very consistent conduct; acquired & ever while she lived maintained a most powerful; & good influence over him. Her plain but kind admonitions generally had the right effect; without arousing his haughty obstinate temper. John began early in life to discover a great liking to fine Cattle, Horses, Sheep, & Swine; & as soon as circumstances would enable him he began to be a practical *Shepherd: it being* a calling for which *in early life* he had a kind of *enthusiastic longing:* together with the idea that as a business it bid fair to afford him the means of carrying out his greatest or principal object. I have now given you a kind of general idea of the early life of this boy; & if I believed it would be worth the trouble; or afford much interest to any good feeling person: I might be tempted to tell you something of his course in after life; or manhood. I do not say that I *will do it.*

You will discover that in using up my *half sheets to save paper;* I have written Two pages, so that one does not follow the other as it should. I have no time to write it over; & but for unavoidable hindrances in traveling I can hardly say when I should have written what I have. With an honest desire for your best good, I subscribe myself,

Your Friend,

J. Brown.

P.S. I had like to have forgotten to acknowledge your contribution in aid of the cause in which I serve. God Almighty *bless you;* my son.

2

Bleeding Kansas: The Crusade Begins

All efforts to understand John Brown must take into account his experiences in the Kansas Territory, for it was there that the pattern of his last four years began to take shape. His notoriety from these years, especially 1856, earned him the nickname of "Osawatomie Brown," and subsequently, by stressing his role as a freedom fighter, Brown attracted the financial and moral support of several prominent easterners for his further exploits. The three documents in this section give disparate impressions of his activities in Kansas. The first is the testimony of James Harris before a congressional investigating committee concerning the so-called Pottawatomie massacre of May 24–25; Harris's cabin was the last of five proslavery homesteads Brown and his men visited that night. Next are Brown's letters to his family in which he denies involvement in this grisly affair, a posture of innocence he maintained for the rest of his life. The letters suggest the violent climate in which Brown operated and the suffering he endured in Kansas, factors which both contemporaries and later commentators would use to explain Brown's subsequent career and conduct.

TESTIMONY OF JAMES HARRIS [1]

On Sunday morning, May 25, 1856, about two A.M., while my wife and child and myself were in bed in the house where we lived, near Henry Sherman's, we were aroused by a company of men who said they belonged to the Northern army, and who were each armed with a sabre and two revolvers, two of whom I recognized; namely, a Mr. Brown, whose given name I do not remember (commonly known by the appellation of "old man Brown"), and his son Owen Brown. They came into the house and approached the bedside

[1] From Franklin B. Sanborn, ed., *The Life and Letters of John Brown* (Boston: Roberts Brothers, 1891), pp. 265–66.

26

where we were lying, and ordered us, together with three other men who were in the same house with me, to surrender; that the Northern army was upon us, and it would be no use for us to resist. The names of these other men who were then in the house with me were William Sherman and John S. Whiteman; the other man I did not know. They were stopping with me that night. They had bought a cow from Henry Sherman, and intended to go home the next morning. When they came up to the bed, some had drawn sabres in their hands, and some revolvers. They then took into their possession two rifles and a bowie-knife, which I had there in the room (there was but one room in my house), and afterwards ransacked the whole establishment in search of ammunition. They then took one of these three men, who were staying in my house, out. (This was the man whose name I did not know.) He came back. They then took me out, and asked me if there were any more men about the place. I told them there were not. They searched the place, but found no others but us four. They asked me where Henry Sherman was. (Henry was a brother to William Sherman.) I told them he was out on the plains in search of some cattle which he had lost. They asked me if I had ever taken any hand in aiding proslavery men in coming to the Territory of Kansas, or had ever taken any hand in the last troubles at Lawrence; they asked me whether I had ever done the Free-State party any harm, or ever intended to do that party any harm; they asked me what made me live at such a place. I then answered that I could get higher wages there than anywhere else. They asked me if there were any bridles or saddles about the premises. I told them there was one saddle, which they took; and they also took possession of Henry Sherman's horse, which I had at my place, and made me saddle him. They then said if I would answer no to all the questions which they has asked me, they would let me loose. Old Mr. Brown and his son then went into the house with me. The other three men—Mr. William Sherman, Mr. Whiteman, and the stranger—were in the house all this time. After old man Brown and his son went into the house with me, old man Brown asked Mr. Sherman to go out with him; and Mr. Sherman then went out with old Mr. Brown, and another man came into the house in Brown's place. I heard nothing more for about fifteen minutes. Two of the Northern army, as they styled themselves, stayed in with us until we heard a cap burst, and then these two men left. That morning, about ten o'clock, I found William Sherman dead in the creek near my house. I was looking for him; as he had not come back, I thought he had been murdered. I took Mr. William Sherman out of the creek and examined him. Mr. Whiteman was with me. Sherman's skull was split open in two places, and some of his brains was washed out by the water. A large hole was cut in his breast, and his left hand was cut off except a little piece of skin on one side. We buried him.

BROWN TO FAMILY, JUNE, 1856 [2]

It is now about five weeks since I have seen a line from North Elba, or had any chance of writing you. During that period we here have passed through an almost constant series of very trying events. We were called to the relief of Lawrence, May 22, and every man (eight in all), except Orson turned out; he staying with the women and children, and to take care of the cattle. John was captain of a company to which Jason belonged; the other six were a little company by ourselves. On our way to Lawrence we learned that it had been already destroyed, and we encamped with John's company overnight. Next day our little company left, and during the day we stopped and searched three men.

Lawrence was destroyed in this way: Their leading men had (as I think) decided, in a very *cowardly* manner, not to resist any process having any Government official to serve it, notwithstanding the process might be wholly a bogus affair. The consequence was that a man called a United States marshal came on with a horde of ruffians which he called his posse, and after arresting a few persons turned the ruffians loose on the defenceless people. They robbed the inhabitants of their money and other property, and even women of their ornaments, and burned considerable of the town.

On the second day and evening after we left John's men we encountered quite a number of proslavery men, and took quite a number prisoners. Our prisoners we let go; but we kept some four or five horses. We were immediately after this accused of murdering five men at Pottawatomie, and great efforts have since been made by the Missourians and their ruffian allies to capture us. John's company soon afterward disbanded, and also the Osawatomie men.

Jason started to go and place himself under the protection of the Government troops; but on his way he was taken prisoner by the Bogus men, and is yet a prisoner, I suppose. John tried to hide for several days; but from feelings of the ungrateful conduct of those who ought to have stood by him, excessive fatigue, anxiety, and

[2] Ibid., pp. 236–41. Footnotes have been omitted.

constant loss of sleep, he became quite insane, and in that situation gave up, or, as we are told, was betrayed at Osawatomie into the hands of the Bogus men. We do not know all the truth about this affair. He has since, we are told, been kept in irons, and brought to a trial before a bogus court, the result of which we have not yet learned. We have great anxiety both for him and Jason, and numerous other prisoners with the enemy (who have all the while had the Government troops to sustain them). We can only commend them to God.

The cowardly mean conduct of Osawatomie and vicinity did not save them; for the ruffians came on them, made numerous prisoners, fired their buildings, and robbed them. After this a picked party of the Bogus men went to Brown's Station, burned John's and Jason's houses, and their contents to ashes; in which burning we have all suffered more or less. Orson and boy have been prisoners, but were soon set at liberty. They are well, and have not been seriously injured. Owen and I have just come here for the first time to look at the ruins. All looks desolate and forsaken,—the grass and weeds fast covering up the signs that these places were lately the abodes of quiet families. After burning the houses, this self-same party of picked men, some forty in number, set out as they supposed, and as was the fact, on the track of my little company, boasting, with awful profanity, that they would have our scalps. They however passed the place where we were hid, and robbed a little town some four or five miles beyond our camp in the timber. I had omitted to say that some murders had been committed at the time Lawrence was sacked. . . .

Since then we have, like David of old, had our dwelling with the serpents of the rocks and wild beasts of the wilderness; being obliged to hide away from our enemies. We are not disheartened, though nearly destitute of food, clothing, and money. God, who has not given us over to the will of our enemies, but has moreover delivered them into our hand, will, we humbly trust, still keep and deliver us. We feel assured that He who sees not as men see, does not lay the guilt of innocent blood to our charge. . . .

BROWN TO FAMILY, SEPTEMBER 7, 1856[3]

I have one moment to write you to say that I am yet alive that Jason & family were well yesterday John; & family I hear are well; (he being yet a prisoner. On the morning of the 30th Aug an attack

---

[3] From the John Brown Papers, Kansas State Historical Society, Topeka, Kansas. Reprinted by permission.

was made by the ruffians on Osawatomie numbering some 400 by whose scouts our dear Fred^k was shot dead without warning he supposing them to be Free State men as near as we can learn. One other man a Cousin of Mr Adair was murdered by them about the same time that Fred^k was killed & one badly wounded at the same time. At this time I was about 3 miles off where I had some 14 or 15 men over night that I had just enlisted to serve under me as regulars. There I collected as well as I could with some 12 or 15 more & in about 3/4 of an Hour attacked them from a wood with thick undergroth., with this force we threw them into confusion for about 15 or 20 Minuets [*sic*] during which time we killed & wounded from 70 to 80 of the enemy *as they say* & then we escaped as well as we could with one killed while escaping; Two or Three wounded; & as many more missing. Four or Five Free State men were butchered during the day in all. Jason fought bravely by my side during the fight & escaped with me he being unhurt. I was struck by a partly spent, Grape, Canister, or Rifle shot which bruised me some but did not injure me seriously. "Hitherto the Lord hath helped me" notwithstanding my afflictions. Things now seem rather quiet just now: but what another Hour will bring I cannot say. . . .

3

"Rail Road Business on a Somewhat Extended Scale"

After Brown left Kansas in the fall of 1856, he returned east to spend part of 1857 in fund raising. He went west again later that year to set up a training school for new recruits, with Hugh Forbes. No one knows the precise stage of the development of his plans as he left Kansas for the second time in December, 1857.

Brown's correspondence deals circumspectly with the evolution of his scheme for a southern invasion. Evidence from others, however, suggests that Brown had contemplated some action against slavery in the South while he was engaged in the wool business in Springfield, Massachusetts. In 1847, Brown revealed to Frederick Douglass a plan to establish a "Subterranean Pass Way" in the Allegheny Mountains through which he could run off slaves to the North. The next reference to this idea appears in a notebook entry of 1857 in which Brown listed four Pennsylvania cities and strategic locations in the South such as Little Rock, Charleston, San Antonio, St. Louis, and Augusta alongside a notation citing the life of Wellington for useful hints in guerrilla warfare. In March of the same year, during his first fund-raising trip in the Northeast, Brown contracted with Charles Blair of Collinsville, Connecticut, for 1,000 pikes, which he later shipped to Harper's Ferry.

Brown's correspondence with his financial supporters in 1858 suggests that his plan was maturing. Although he first mentioned Harper's Ferry in an April 8 letter to his son John Jr., he had evidently chosen the location some months earlier. Whether the so-called Secret Six knew the dimensions of Brown's scheme in detail is still unknown and was a subject of intense controversy after the raid.

FREDERICK DOUGLASS ON HIS RELATIONSHIP WITH BROWN [1]

*Unlike most materials in Parts One and Two, the selections
from Douglass are not contemporary accounts but later recollections published in his autobiography.*

What was my connection with John Brown, and what I knew
of his scheme for the capture of Harper's Ferry, I may now proceed
to state. From the time of my visit to him in Springfield, Mass., in
1847, our relations were friendly and confidential. I never passed
through Springfield without calling on him, and he never came to
Rochester without calling on me. He often stopped over night with
me, when we talked over the feasibility of his plan for destroying
the value of slave property, and the motive for holding slaves in the
border States. That plan, as already intimated elsewhere, was to
take twenty or twenty-five discreet and trustworthy men into the
mountains of Virginia and Maryland, and station them in squads
of five, about five miles apart, on a line of twenty-five miles; each
squad to co-operate with all, and all with each. They were to have
selected for them, secure and comfortable retreats in the fastnesses
of the mountains, where they could easily defend themselves in case
of attack. They were to subsist upon the country roundabout. They
were to be well armed, but were to avoid battle or violence, unless
compelled by pursuit or in self-defense. In that case, they were to
make it as costly as possible to the assailing party, whether that
party should be soldiers or citizens. He further proposed to have a
number of stations from the line of Pennsylvania to the Canada
border, where such slaves as he might, through his men, induce to
run away, should be supplied with food and shelter and be for-
warded from one station to another till they should reach a place
of safety either in Canada or the Northern States. He proposed to
add to his force in the mountains any courageous and intelligent
fugitives who might be willing to remain and endure the hardships
and brave the dangers of this mountain life. These, he thought, if
properly selected, on account of their knowledge of the surrounding
country, could be made valuable auxiliaries. The work of going
into the valley of Virginia and persuading the slaves to flee to the

[1] From Frederick Douglass, *Life and Times of Frederick Douglass* (Hartford,
Conn.: Park Publishing Co., 1881), pp. 318–21.

mountains, was to be committed to the most courageous and judicious man connected with each squad.

Hating slavery as I did, and making its abolition the object of my life, I was ready to welcome any new mode of attack upon the slave system which gave any promise of success. I readily saw that this plan could be made very effective in rendering slave property in Maryland and Virginia valueless by rendering it insecure. Men do not like to buy runaway horses, nor to invest their money in a species of property likely to take legs and walk off with itself. In the worse case, too, if the plan should fail, and John Brown should be driven from the mountains, a new fact would be developed by which the nation would be kept awake to the existence of slavery. Hence, I assented to this, John Brown's scheme or plan for running off slaves.

To set this plan in operation, money and men, arms and ammunition, food and clothing, were needed; and these, from the nature of the enterprise, were not easily obtained, and nothing was immediately done. Captain Brown, too, notwithstanding his rigid economy, was poor, and was unable to arm and equip men for the dangerous life he had mapped out. So the work lingered till after the Kansas trouble was over, and freedom was a fact accomplished in that Territory. This left him with arms and men, for the men who had been with him in Kansas, believed in him, and would follow him in any humane but dangerous enterprise he might undertake.

After the close of his Kansas work, Captain Brown came to my house in Rochester, and said he desired to stop with me several weeks; "but," he added, "I will not stay unless you will allow me to pay board." Knowing that he was no trifler and meant all he said, and desirous of retaining him under my roof, I charged three dollars a week. While here, he spent most of his time in correspondence. He wrote often to George L. Stearns of Boston, Gerrit Smith of Peterboro, N. Y., and many others, and received many letters in return. When he was not writing letters, he was writing and revising a constitution which he meant to put in operation by the men who should go with him in the mountains. He said that to avoid anarchy and confusion, there should be a regularly constituted government, to which each man who came with him should be sworn to honor and support. I have a copy of this constitution in Captain Brown's own handwriting, as prepared by himself at my house.

He called his friends from Chatham (Canada) to come together that he might lay his constitution before them, for their approval and adoption. His whole time and thought were given to this subject. It was the first thing in the morning and the last thing at night, till I confess it began to be something of a bore to me. Once in a while he would say he could, with a few resolute men, capture Harper's Ferry, and supply himself with arms belonging to the government at that place, but he never announced his intention to do so. It was however, very evidently passing in his mind as a thing he might do. I paid but little attention to such remarks, though I never doubted that he thought just what he said. Soon after his coming to me, he asked me to get for him two smoothly planed boards, upon which he could illustrate, with a pair of dividers, by a drawing, the plan of fortification which he meant to adopt in the mountains.

These forts were to be so arranged as to connect one with the other, by secret passages, so that if one was carried, another could easily be fallen back upon, and be the means of dealing death to the enemy at the very moment when he might think himself victorious. I was less interested in these drawings than my children were, but they showed that the old man had an eye to the means as well as to the end, and was giving his best thought to the work he was about to take in hand.

It was his intention to begin this work in '58 instead of '59. . . .

BROWN TO THEODORE PARKER, FEBRUARY 2, 1858 [2]

I am again out of Kansas, and am at this time concealing my whereabouts; but for very different reasons, however, from those I had for doing so at Boston last spring. I have nearly perfected arrangements for carrying out an important measure in which the world has a deep interest, as well as Kansas; and only lack from five to eight hundred dollars to enable me to do so,—the same object for which I asked for secret-service money last fall. It is my only errand here; and I have written to some of our mutual friends in regard to it, but they none of them understand my views so well as you do, and I cannot explain without their first committing themselves more than I know of their doing. I have heard that Parker Pillsbury and some others in your quarter hold out ideas similar to those on which I act; but I have no personal acquaintance with them, and know nothing of their influence or means. Cannot you either by direct or indirect action do something to further me? Do you not

[2] Sanborn, *John Brown*, pp. 434–35.

know of some parties whom you could induce to give their abolition theories a thoroughly practical shape? I hope this will prove to be the last time I shall be driven to harass a friend in such a way. Do you think any of my Garrisonian friends, either at Boston, Worcester, or any other place, can be induced to supply a little "straw," if I will absolutely make "bricks"? I have written George L. Stearns, Esq., of Medford, and Mr. F. B. Sanborn, of Concord; but I am not informed as to how deeply-dyed Abolitionists those friends are, and must beg you to consider this communication strictly confidential,—unless you know of parties who will feel and act, and hold their peace. I want to bring the thing about during the next sixty days. Please write N. Hawkins, care William J. Watkins, Esq., Rochester, N. Y.

BROWN TO THOMAS WENTWORTH HIGGINSON, FEBRUARY 2, 1858 [3]

I am here *concealing my whereabouts* for good reasons (as I think) not however from any anxiety about my personal safety. I have been told that you are both a true *man:* & a true *abolitionist* "& I partly believe" the whole story. Last Fall I undertook to raise from $500 to $1,000, for *secret service,* & succeeded in getting $500. I now want to get for the *perfecting* of *by far* the most *important* undertaking of my whole life: from $500 to $800 within the next sixty days. I have written Rev Theodore Parker, George L Stearns, & F B Sanborn Esq, on the subject; but do not know as either Mr Stearns or Mr Sanborn, are abolitionists. I suppose they are. Can you be induced to operate at Worcester, & elsewhere during that time to raise from *Anti*slavery *men* & *women,* (or any other parties) some part of that amount? I wish to keep it entirely still about where I am: & will be *greatly obliged* if you will consider this communication *strictly confidential:* unless it maybe with such as you are *sure* will *feel,* & *act,* & *keep very still.* Please be so kind as to write N Hawkins on the subject care of Wm. L. Watkins Esq., Rochester New York. Should be most happy to meet you again; & talk matters more freely. Hope this is my last effort in the begging line.

[3] From the Thomas Wentworth Higginson Papers in the Boston Public Library, Boston, Massachusetts. Reprinted by permission.

T. W. HIGGINSON TO N. HAWKINS (BROWN), FEBRUARY 8, 1858 [4]

I am always ready to invest money in treason, but at present have none to invest. As for my friends, those who are able are not quite willing, and those who are willing are at present bankrupt. Beside this, I have most of our fugitives to look after, & have just undertaken to raise something for the Underground Railroad in Kansas, which is in full operation just now. But I'll raise something, if only $5 &, send it on. I may be able to persuade our Committee who have a trifling balance left.

F. B. SANBORN TO T. W. HIGGINSON, FEBRUARY 11, 1858 [5]

I have received two letters from J. B. in which he speaks of *a* plan but does not say what it is. Still I have confidence enough in him to trust him with the moderate sum he asks for—if I had it—without knowing his plan—Morton writes me from Gerrit Smith's that with from 5 to 800 $ J. B. hopes to do more than has yet been done; wishes to raise the money in two months—Meanwhile he is staying up with Douglass (Fred) at Rochester, and avoids publicity as much as possible. In his last letter he says he shall probably continue to see me—and I think he will be in Boston before long—He expects "to overthrow slavery in a large part of the country." E. B. Whitman writes me from Lawrence that Brown has disappeared and has been of little service to them—adding that some say he is insane—

This—of course is not so—If you can aid Brown in any substantial way please do so—for I do not well see how I can, though I shall try—Mr Smith has sent him $100—Has B. written to you? I judge so—I should not wonder if his plan contemplates an uprising of slaves—though he has not said as much to me—

The Union is evidently on its last legs and Buchannan is laboring to tear it in pieces—Treason will not be treason much longer, but patriotism—

Write me if you can do anything for B—

Is it true that [?] is going to Syracuse?

[4] Ibid.
[5] Ibid.

BROWN TO T. W. HIGGINSON, ROCHESTER, NEW YORK, FEBRUARY 12, 1858 [6]

I have just read your kind letter of the 8th instant, & will now say that Rail Road business on a *somewhat extended scale,* is the *identical* object for which I am trying to get means. I have been connected with that business *as commonly conducted* from my boyhood &, *never* let an opportunity slip. I have been opperating to some purpose *the past season:* but I now have a measure on *foot* that I feel *sure* would awaken in you something more than a *common interest;* if you could understand it. I have just written my friends G L Stearns, & F B Sanborn, asking them to meet me for consultation at Gerrit Smiths, Peterboro. I am very anxious to have *you come along; certain as I feel;* that you will never regret having been one of the council. I would most gladly pay your expenses had I the means to spare. *Will you come on?* Please write as before.

BROWN TO F. B. SANBORN, FEBRUARY 24, 1858 [7]

Mr. Morton has taken the liberty of saying to me that you felt half inclined to make a common cause with me. I greatly rejoice at this; for I believe when you come to look at the ample field I labor in, and the rich harvest which not only this entire country but the whole world during the present and future generations may reap from its successful cultivation, you will feel that you are out of your element until you find you are in it, an entire unit. What an inconceivable amount of good you might so effect by your counsel, your example, your encouragement, your natural and acquired ability for active service! And then, how very little we can possibly lose! Certainly the cause is enough to *live* for, if not to —— for. I have only had this one opportunity, in a life of nearly sixty years; and could I be continued ten times as long again, I might not again have another equal opportunity. God has honored but comparatively a very small part of mankind with any possible chance for such mighty and soul-satisfying rewards. But, my dear friend, if you should make up your mind to do so, I trust it will be wholly from the promptings of your own spirit, after having

[6] Ibid.
[7] Sanborn, *John Brown,* pp. 444–45.

thoroughly counted the cost. I would flatter no man into such a measure, if I could do it ever so easily.

I expect nothing but to "endure hardness"; but I expect to effect a mighty conquest, even though it be like the last victory of Samson. I felt for a number of years, in earlier life, a steady, strong desire to die; but since I saw any prospect of becoming a "reaper" in the great harvest, I have not only felt quite willing to live, but have enjoyed life much; and am now rather anxious to live for a few years more.

BROWN TO HIS WIFE, MARY, MARCH 2, 1858 [8]

I received yours of the 17th of February yesterday; was very glad of it, and to know that you had got the ten dollars safe. I am having a constant series of both great encouragements and discouragements, but am yet able to say, in view of all, "hitherto the Lord hath helped me." I shall send Salmon something as soon as I can, and will try to get you the articles you mention. I find a much more earnest feeling among the colored people than ever before; but that is by no means unusual. On the whole, the language of Providence to me would certainly seem to say, "Try on." I flatter myself that I may be able to go and see you again before a great while; but I may not be able. I long to see you all. All were well with John and Jason a few days since. I had a good visit with Mr. Sanborn at Gerrit Smith's a few days ago. It would be no very strange thing if he should join me. May God abundantly bless you all! No one writes me but you.

BROWN TO THEODORE PARKER, MARCH 7, 1858 [9]

Since you know I have an almost countless brood of poor hungry chickens to "scratch for," you will not reproach me for scratching even on the Sabbath. At any rate, I trust God will not. I want you to undertake to provide a substitute for an address you saw last season, directed to the officers and soldiers of the United States Army. The ideas contained in that address I of course like, for I furnished the skeleton. I never had the ability to clothe those ideas in language at all to satisfy myself; and I was by no means satisfied with the style of that address, and do not know as I can give any correct idea of what I want. I will, however, try.

[8] Ibid., pp. 442–43.
[9] Ibid., pp. 448–49.

In the first place it must be short, or it will not be generally read. It must be in the simplest or plainest language, without the least affectation of the scholar about it, and yet be worded with great clearness and power. The anonymous writer must (in the language of the Paddy) be "afther others," and not "afther himself at all, at all." If the spirit that communicated Franklin's Poor Richard (or some other good spirit) would dictate, I think it would be quite as well employed as the "dear sister spirits" have been for some years past. The address should be appropriate, and particularly adapted to the peculiar circumstances we anticipate, and should look to the actual change of service from that of Satan to the service of God. It should be, in short, a most earnest and powerful appeal to men's sense of right and to their feelings of humanity. Soldiers are men, and no man can certainly calculate the value and importance of getting a single "nail into old Captain Kidd's chest." It should be provided beforehand, and be ready in advance to distribute by all persons, male and female, who may be disposed to favor the right.

I also want a similar short address, appropriate to the peculiar circumstances, intended for all persons, old and young, male and female, slaveholding and non-slaveholding, to be sent out broadcast over the entire nation. So by every male and female prisoner on being set at liberty, and to be read by them during confinement. I know that men will listen, and reflect too, under such circumstances. Persons will hear your antislavery lectures and abolition lectures when they have become virtually slaves themselves. The impressions made on prisoners by kindness and plain dealing, instead of barbarous and cruel treatment, such as they might give, and instead of being slaughtered like wild reptiles, as they might very naturally expect, are not only powerful but lasting. Females are susceptible of being carried away entirely by the kindness of an intrepid and magnanimous soldier, even when his bare name was but a terror the day previous. Now, dear sir, I have told you about as well as I know how, what I am anxious at once to secure. Will you write the tracts, or get them written, so that I may commence colporteur?

A PORTION OF A LETTER FROM BROWN TO JOHN BROWN, JR., APRIL 8, 1858 [10]

I came on here direct with J. W. Loguen the day after you left Rochester. I am succeeding, to all appearance, beyond my expecta-

---

[10] Ibid., p. 452.

tions. Harriet Tubman hooked on his whole team at once. He (Harriet) is the most of a man, naturally, that I ever met with. There is the most abundant material, and of the right quality, in this quarter, beyond all doubt. Do not forget to write Mr. Case (near Rochester) at once about hunting up every person and family of the reliable kind about, at, or near Bedford, Chambersburg, Gettysburg, and Carlisle, in Pennsylvania, and also Hagerstown and vicinity, Maryland, and *Harper's Ferry, Va.* The names and residences of all, I want to have sent me at Lindenville.

4

Preparations and Pronouncements

*In late April, 1858, Brown and twelve of his fol-
lowers journeyed to Chatham, Canada, a town of 6,000 resi-
dents, a third of whom were fugitive slaves. There Brown
called a convention to consider his Provisional Constitution,
which was designed to create a new state in the captured slave-
holding territory. Although disappointed by the small turnout
(none of the Secret Six attended), Brown had the pleasure of
seeing his Constitution adopted and himself elected Commander-in-Chief of its army. Virtually all of the thirty-four
blacks present signed the Constitution; however few volunteered to join Brown's small force.*

*Just how much of his plan he divulged to the convention
membership is unknown; at least one participant, prominent
Negro Dr. Martin R. Delany, writing in 1868, claimed that
Kansas, not the southern states, was the object of his plans.
The confession given by John Cook after the raid stated that
Brown had announced the Harper's Ferry destination to his
dozen men in the fall of 1857, but did not claim that the con-
vention delegates knew of it.*

*Although the exact date is uncertain, Richard Hinton sug-
gested that "The Declaration of Liberty by Representatives
of the Slave Population of the U.S.A." was written at or
shortly after Chatham. It is included here as a vivid statement
of Brown's attitude toward the institution of slavery.*

THE ACCOUNT OF THE CHATHAM CONVENTION
BY DR. MARTIN R. DELANY [1]

. . . [John Brown] revealed to me that he desired to carry
out a great project in his scheme of Kansas emigration, which, to
be successful, must be aided and countenanced by the influence of

[1] From Richard J. Hinton, *John Brown and His Men: With Some Account of
the Roads They Traveled to Reach Harper's Ferry* (New York: Funk & Wagnalls
Company, 1894), pp. 715–18.

a general convention or council. *That* he was unable to effect in the United States, but had been advised by distinguished friends of his and mine, that, if he could but see me, his object could be attained at once. On my expressing astonishment at the conclusion to which my friends and himself had arrived, with a nervous impatience, he exclaimed, "Why should you be surprised? Sir, the people of the Northern States are cowards; slavery has made cowards of them all. The whites are afraid of each other, and the blacks are afraid of the whites. You can effect nothing among such people," he added, with decided emphasis. On assuring him if a council were all that was desired, he could readily obtain it, he replied, "That is all; but that is a great deal to me. It is men I want, and not money; money I can get plentiful enough, but no men. Money can come without being seen, but men are afraid of identification with me, though they favor my measures. They are cowards, sir! cowards!" he reiterated. He then fully revealed his designs. With these I found no fault, but fully favored and aided in getting up the convention.

The convention, when assembled, consisted of Captain John Brown, his son Owen, eleven or twelve of his Kansas followers, all young white men, enthusiastic and able, and probably sixty or seventy colored men, whom I brought together.

His plans were made known to them as soon as he was satisfied that the assemblage could be confided in, which conclusion he was not long in finding, for with few exceptions the whole of these were fugitive slaves, refugees in her Britannic majesty's dominion. His scheme was nothing more than this: To make Kansas, instead of Canada, the terminus of the Underground Railroad; instead of passing off the slave to Canada, to send him to Kansas, and there test, on the soil of the United States territory, whether or not the right of freedom would be maintained where no municipal power had authorized.

He stated that he had originated a fortification so simple, that twenty men, without the aid of teams or ordnance, could build one in a day that would defy all the artillery that could be brought to bear against it. How it was constructed he would not reveal, and none knew it except his great confidential officer, Kagi (the secretary of war in his contemplated provisional government), a young lawyer of marked talents and singular demeanor.

Major Delany stated that he had proposed, as a cover to the change in the scheme, as Canada had always been known as the terminus of the Underground Railroad, and pursuit of the fugitive was made in that direction, to call it the Subterranean Pass Way, where the initials would stand S. P. W., to note the direction in which he had gone when not sent to Canada. He further stated that the idea of Harper's Ferry was never mentioned, or even hinted in that convention.

Had such been intimated, it is doubtful of its being favorably regarded. Kansas, where he had battled so valiantly for freedom, seemed the proper place for his vantage-ground, and the kind and condition of men for whom he had fought, the men with whom to fight. Hence the favor which the scheme met of making Kansas the terminus of the Subterranean Pass Way, and there fortifying with these fugitives against the border slaveholders, for personal liberty, with which they had no right to interfere. Thus it is clearly explained that it was no design against the Union, as the slaveholders and their satraps interpreted the movement, and by this means would anticipate their designs.

This also explains the existence of the constitution for a civil government found in the carpet-bag among the effects of Captain Brown, after his capture in Virginia. . . .

This organization was an extensive body, holding the same relation to his movements as a state or national executive committee hold to its party principles, directing their adherence to fundamental principles.

This, he says, was the plan and purpose of the Canada Convention, whatever changed them to Harper's Ferry was known only to Captain Brown, and perhaps to Kagi, who had the honor of being deeper in his confidence than any one else. Mr. Osborn Anderson, one of the survivors of that immortal band, and whose statement as one of the principal actors in that historical drama cannot be ignored, states that none of the men knew that Harper's Ferry was the point of attack until the order was given to march.

PORTIONS OF JOHN COOK'S "CONFESSION," NOVEMBER, 1859[2]

A young member of Brown's raiding party who had joined Brown in Kansas in 1857 was John Cook. His confession was made in Charlestown at the suggestion of his lawyer, in an effort to save his life. After describing his initial work with

[2] Ibid., pp. 702–705.

*Brown in Kansas, Cook went on to describe how the Harper's
Ferry scheme developed.*

. . . We stopped some days at Tabor, making preparations
to start. Here we found that Captain Brown's ultimate destination
was the State of Virginia. Some warm words passed between him
and myself in regard to the plan, which I had supposed was to be
confined entirely to Kansas and Missouri. Realf and Parsons were
of the same opinion with me. After a good deal of wrangling we
consented to go on, as we had not the means to return, and the rest
of the party were so anxious that we should go with them. . . .
. . . We remained at Pedee [Springfield, Iowa] till about the
middle of April, when we left for Chatham, Canada, *via* Chicago
and Detroit. We staid about two weeks in Chatham—some of the
party staid six or seven weeks. We left Chatham for Cleveland, and
remained there until late in June. In the meantime, Captain
Brown went East on business; but previous to his departure he
had learned that Colonel Forbes had betrayed his plans to some
extent. This, together with the scantiness of his funds, induced
him to delay the commencement of his work, and was the means,
for the time being, of disbanding the party. He had also received
some information which called for his immediate attention in
Kansas. I wished to go with him, but he said that I was too well
known there, and requested me and some others to go to Harper's
Ferry, Va., to see how things were there, and to gain information.
While we were in Chatham he called a convention, the purpose of
which was to make a complete and thorough organization. He
issued a written circular, which he sent to various persons in the
United States and Canada. . . .
  As the names were left blank I do not know to whom they were
sent, though I wrote several of them. I learned, however, that one
was sent to Frederick Douglass, and I think Gerrit Smith also
received one. Who the others were sent to I do not know. Neither
Douglass nor Smith attended the convention. I suppose some
twenty-five or thirty of these circulars were sent, but as they were
directed by Captain Brown or J. H. Kagi I do not know the names
of the parties to whom they were addressed. I do know, however,
that they were sent to none save those whom Captain Brown knew
to be radical abolitionists. I think it was about ten days from the

time the circulars were sent that the convention met. The place of meeting was in one of the negro churches in Chatham. The convention, I think, was called to order by J. H. Kagi. Its object was then stated, which was to complete a thorough organization and the formation of a constitution. The first business was to elect a president and secretary. Elder Monroe, a colored minister, was elected President, and J. H. Kagi, Secretary. The next business was to form a constitution. Captain Brown had already drawn up one, which, on motion, was read by the Secretary. On motion it was ordered that each article of the constitution be taken up and separately amended and passed, which was done. On motion, the constitution was then adopted as a whole. The next business was to nominate a Commander-in-Chief, Secretary of War, and Secretary of State. Captain John Brown was unanimously elected Commander-in-Chief; J. H. Kagi, Secretary of War, and Richard Realf, Secretary of State. Elder Monroe was to act as President until another was chosen. A. M. Chapman, I think, was to act as Vice-President. Doctor M. K. Delany was one of the Corresponding Secretaries of the organization. There were some others from the United States, whose names I do not now remember. Most of the delegates to the Convention were from Canada. After the constitution was adopted, the members took their oath to support it. It was then signed by all present. During the interval between the call for the convention and its assembling, regular meetings were held at Barbour's Hotel, where we were stopping, by those who were known to be true to the cause, at which meetings plans were laid and discussed. There were no white men at the convention save the members of our company. Men and money had both been promised from Chatham and other parts of Canada. When the convention broke up, news was received that Col. H. Forbes, who had joined in the movement, had given information to the government. This, of course, delayed the time of attack. A day or two afterward most of our party took the boat to Cleveland—Jno. H. Kagi, Richard Realf, Wm. H. Leeman, Richard Robertson, and Capt. Brown remaining. Capt. B., however, started in a day or two for the East. Kagi, I think, returned to some other town in Canada, to set up the type and to get the constitution printed, which he completed before he went to Cleveland. We remained in Cleveland for some weeks, at which place, for the time being, the company disbanded. Capt. Brown had had the plan of the insurrection in contemplation for several years—in fact, told me that it had been the chief aim of his life to carry out and accomplish the abolition of slavery. . . .

"A DECLARATION OF LIBERTY BY THE REPRESENTATIVES OF THE SLAVE POPULATION OF THE UNITED STATES OF AMERICA "[3]

When in the course of Human events, it becomes necessary for an oppressed People to Rise, and assert their Natural Rights, as Human Beings, as Native and Mutual Citizens of a free Republic, and break that odious yoke of oppression, which is so unjustly laid upon them by their fellow countrymen, and to assume among the powers of Earth the same equal privileges to which the Laws of Nature, and nature's God entitle, them; A moderate respect for the opinions of Mankind, requires that they should declare the causes which incite them to this Just & worthy action.

We hold these truths to be Self Evident; That all men are created Equal; That they are endowed by the Creator with certain unalienable rights. That among these are Life, Liberty; & pursuit of happiness. . . .

The history of Slavery in the United States, is a history of injustice and cruelties inflicted upon the Slave in every conceivable way, and in barbarity not surpassed by the most savage Tribes. It is the embodiment of all that is Evil, and ruinous to a Nation; and subversive of all Good. In proof of which; facts innumerable have been submitted to the People, and have received the verdict and condemnation of a candid and Impartial World. Our Servants; Members of Congress; and other servants of the People, who receive exorbitant wages, from the People; in return for their unjust Rule, have refused to pass laws for the accommodation of large districts of People, unless that People, would relinquish the right of representation in the Legislation, a right inestimable of them, and formidable to tyrants only. Our President and other Leeches have called together legislative, or treasonable Bodies, at places unusual, uncomfortable, and distant from the depository of our public records; for the sole purpose of fatigueing us into compliance with their measures. They have desolved Representative houses, for opposing with manly firmness, their invasions of the rights of the people.

They have refused to grant Petitions presented by numerous and

[3] Ibid., pp. 637–40, 642–43.

respectable Citizens, asking redress of grivances imposed upon us, demanding our Liberty and natural rights. With contempt they spurn our humble petitions; and have failed to pass laws for our relief. . . . They have abdicated government among us, by declaring us out of their protection, and waging a worse than cruel war upon us continually.

The facts and full description of the enormous sin of Slavery, may be found in the General History of American Slavery, which is a history of repeated injuries, of base hypocracy; A cursed treasonable, usurpation; The most abominable provoking atrocities; which are but a mockery of all that is Just, or worthy of any people. Such cruelty, tyrany, and perfidy, has hardly a parallel, in the history of the most barbarous ages.

Our Servants, or Law makers; are totally unworthy the name of Half Civilized Men. All their National acts, (which apply to slavery,) are false, to the words Spirit, and intention, of the Constitution of the United States, and the Declaration of Independence. . . .

In every stage of these oppressions, we have petitioned for redress, in the most humble terms, Our repeated petitions have been answered only by repeated Injury. A Class of oppressors, whose character is thus marked by every act which may define a Tyranical Despotism, is unfit to rule any People. Nor have we been wanting in attention, to our oppressors; We have warned them from time to time, of attempts (made by their headlong Blindness,) to perpetrate, extend, strengthen, and revive the dieing eliments of this cursed Institution. We have reminded them of our unhappy condition, and of their Cruelties. We have appealed to their native Justice and magnanimity, we have conjured them by the ties of our common nature, our Brotherhood, & common Parentage, to disavow these usurpations, which have destroyed our Kindred friendship, and endangered their safety. They have been Deaf to the voice of Justice & Consanguinity. We must therefore acquiece in the necessity, which denounces their tyrany & unjust rule over us. Declaring that we will serve them no longer as slaves, knowing that the "Laborer is worthy of his hire." We therefore, the Representatives of the circumscribed citizens of the United States, of America in General Congress assembled, appealing to the supreme Judge of the World, for the rectitude of our intentions, Do in the name, & by authority of the oppressed Citizens of the Slave States, Solemnly publish and Declare; that the Slaves are, & of right ought to be as free & and independent as the unchangable Law of God, requires that All Men Shall be. That they are absolved from all allegiance to those Tyrants, who still presist in forcibly subjecting them to perpetual Bondage, and that all friendly connection between them & such Tyrants, is, & ought to be totally desolved, And that as free, & independent citizens of these states, they have a perfect right, a sufficient & just cause, to defend themselves against the tyrany of their oppressors. To solicit aid from & ask the protection of all true friends of humanity & reform, of whatever nation, & wherever found; A right to contract Alliances, & to do all other acts & things which free independent Citizens may of right do. And for the support of Declaration; with a firm reliance on the protection of Devine Providence; We mutually Pledge to each other, Our Lives, and Our Sacred Honor. Indeed; I tremble for my Country, when I reflect; that God is Just; And that his Justice; will not sleep forever &c. &c. Nature is morning for its murdered, and Afflicted Children. Hung be the Heavens in Scarlet.

5
Postponement and Diversion

*On April 27, on the eve of the Chatham conven-
tion, Brown wrote his wife that his sons at North Elba would
"probably be called on before the middle of May." Brown's
timetable for action was altered, however, when Hugh Forbes,
the drillmaster with whom he had quarreled and broken,
made a surprisingly detailed disclosure of the plan to Massachusetts Senator Henry Wilson and others in early May.
Forbes's May 14 letter to Howe set off a frenzied exchange
among the Secret Six, who feared that their own involvement
with Brown would be made public. Howe and Higginson
wanted Brown to go forward with his plan anyway, but the
more cautious Parker, Stearns, Smith, and Sanborn urged
postponement for a year. Brown made a hurried trip to Boston to argue against delay, but was unsuccessful. Because
Stearns and Smith, in particular, were the major sources of
funds, Brown reluctantly accepted their advice to undertake
diversionary action in Kansas and remain there until the
spring of 1859.*

T. W. HIGGINSON TO BROWN, MAY 7, 1858 [1]

Sanborn writes an alarming letter of a certain H[ugh].
F[orbes]. who wishes to veto our veteran friends project entirely.
Who the man is I have no conception—but I utterly protest against
any postponement. *If the thing is postponed, it is postponed for
ever*—for H. F. can do as much harm next year as this. His malice
must be in some way put down or *outwitted*—& after the move is
once begun, his plots will be of little importance. I believe that we
have gone too far to go back without certain failure, & I believe
our friend the veteran will think so too.

[1] From the Higginson Papers, Boston Public Library. Reprinted by permission.

F. B. SANBORN TO T. W. HIGGINSON, MAY 11, 1858 [2]

I enclose a letter from Gerrit Smith, whose view of the matter agrees with that of our Boston friends. There is much force in your arguments but I cannot quite yield to them, though I wish I could. F. has it in his power to remove the terror of the thing by a complete exposure of the small resources of the group and thus it would lose its main strength—Whether he is base enough to do this I still doubt—but the risk is too great to run—A year hence we may get him over the water where he will know less of movements here and have less means to undermine confidence—while he may be induced to believe that all has been thrown up, and so put off the batch of disclosures—

But his preaching now would spoil the scheme forever since very similar movement would be suspected and watched closely.

I am glad you stand so strongly for the other side—for the matter will thus be fairly argued—but I think when H[owe]. comes to see F.'s letters and knows how minute his information is, he will attach more importance to his opposition than he did on the 5th of May when he wrote me saying he would go on if supplies did not fail him. But the opinion of P[arker]., H[owe]., and S[mith].—and of G[eorge]. S[tearns]. who are such large stockholders will prevent their raising money now and the rest of us can do little in that way——

PORTION OF A LETTER FROM HUGH FORBES TO DR. SAMUEL G. HOWE, MAY 14, 1858 [3]

No preparatory notice having been given to the slaves (no notice could go or with prudence be given them) the invitation to rise might, unless they were already in a state of agitation, meet with no response, or a feeble one. To this Brown replied that he was sure of a response. He calculated that he could get on the first night from 200 to 500. Half, or thereabouts, of this first lot he proposed to keep with him, mounting 100 or so of them, and make a dash at Harper's Ferry manufactory destroying what he could not carry off. The other men not of this party were to be sub-divided into three, four or five distinct parties, each under two or three of the

[2] Ibid.
[3] From *New York Herald*, October 27, 1859.

original band and would beat up other slave quarters whence more men would be sent to join him.

He argued that were he pressed by the U.S. troops, which after a few weeks might concentrate, he could easily maintain himself in the Alleghenies and that his New England partisans would in the meantime call a Northern Convention, restore tranquility and overthrow the pro-slavery administration. This, I contended, could at most be a mere local explosion. A slave insurrection, being from the very nature of things deficient in men of education and experience would under such a system as B. proposed be either a flash in the pan or would leap beyond his control, or any control, when it would become a scene of mere anarchy and would assuredly be suppressed. On the other hand, B. considered foreign intervention as not impossible. As to the dream of a Northern Convention, I considered it as a settled fallacy. Brown's New England friends would not have courage to show themselves, so long as the issue was doubtful, see my letter to J. B. dated 23 February.

BROWN TO F. B. SANBORN, MAY 14, 1858 [4]

Your much-prized letter of the 10th inst. is received. I have only time to say at this moment that as it is an invariable rule with me to be governed by circumstances, or, in other words, not to do anything while I do not know what to do, none of our friends need have any fears in relation to hasty or rash steps being taken by us. As knowledge is said to be power, we propose to become possessed of more knowledge. We have many reasons for begging our Eastern friends to keep clear of F. personally, unless he throws himself upon them. We have those who are thoroughly posted up to put on his track, and we beg to be allowed to do so. We also beg our friends to supply us with three or four hundred dollars without delay, pledging ourselves not to act other than to secure perfect knowledge of facts in regard to what F. has really done, or will do, so that we may ourselves know how we ought to act. None of us here or with you should be hasty, or decide the course to be taken, while under excitement. "In all thy ways acknowledge Him, and He shall direct thy paths." A good cause is sure to be safe in the hands of an all-good, all-wise, and all-powerful Director and Father. Dear Sir, please send this to the friends at Boston and Worcester at once; and in the mean time send me on a plain copy of all that

---

[4] Sanborn, *John Brown*, pp. 456–57.

F. may hereafter write and say. The copy, together with fifteen dollars, is received. Direct all communications on outside envelope to James M. Bell, Chatham, Canada West; the inside, sealed, to Jason Brown.

P. S. You can say with perfect truth to F. that you do not know what has become of me; and you might ask him when he last heard from me, and where I was at the time.

GERRIT SMITH TO F. B. SANBORN, JULY 26, 1858 [5]

I have your letter of the 23d instant. I have great faith in the wisdom, integrity, and bravery of Captain Brown. For several years I have frequently given him money toward sustaining him in his contests with the slave-power. Whenever he shall embark in another of these contests I shall again stand ready to help him; and I will begin with giving him a hundred dollars. I do not wish to know Captain Brown's plans; I hope he will keep them to himself. Can you not visit us this summer? We shall be very glad to see you.

[5] Ibid., p. 466.

6
Versions of the Plan

In June, 1858, a disappointed Brown made his way back to Kansas. In early August, journalist Richard Hinton interviewed Brown and his chief aide, John Henrie Kagi. Kagi revealed to him the status of the plan held in abeyance since Forbes's disclosures. For the next six months Brown remained in Kansas, engaging in guerrilla activity that culminated in a raid into Missouri in December to free slaves. In January, 1859, he left the territory with the fugitives and led them to Canada. Then the old man returned to the East.

In May, Brown met again with the Secret Six in Boston and received encouragement to go forward with his plan. After some success in raising funds, Brown paid a final visit to his family in North Elba in June before departing for Harper's Ferry. He arrived in the Harper's Ferry region on July 3 and soon rented the Kennedy farmhouse in nearby Maryland. In late August he met secretly with Frederick Douglass in Chambersburg, Pennsylvania. There he revealed the full details of the Harper's Ferry plan to the Negro leader. Douglass expressed severe reservations and warned Brown that he was "going into a perfect steel trap, and that once in would never get out alive." Despite Brown's pleas, Douglass refused to join the expedition.

RICHARD J. HINTON'S INTERVIEW WITH JOHN BROWN AND JOHN KAGI [1]

After dinner Kagi had some conversation with the Captain apart. He then asked me if I would walk down to the Marais des Cygnes, "as he was going to fish." I acquiesced, and we started. About half way to the river we stopped and sat on a fence. Kagi asked me what I supposed was the plan of Captain Brown. My answer was, that I thought it had a reference to the Indian Territory and the Southwestern States. He shook his head, and gradually un-

---

[1] From Richard J. Hinton, *John Brown and His Men* (New York: Funk & Wagnalls Company, 1894), pp. 672–75.

folded the whole of their plans. . . . A full account of the conversation in Canada was given, as well as of the organization, its extent and objects, thereby effected. The mountains of Virginia were named as the place of refuge, and as a country admirably adapted to carrying on a guerilla warfare. In the course of the conversation, Harper's Ferry was mentioned as a point to be seized—but not held —on account of the arsenal. The white members of the company were to act as officers of different guerilla bands, which, under the general command of John Brown, were to be composed of Canadian refugees and the Virginia slaves who would join them. A different time of the year was mentioned for the commencement of the warfare from that which has lately been chosen. It was not anticipated that the first movement would have any other appearance to the masters than a slave stampede, or local outbreak at most. The planters would pursue their chattels and be defeated. The militia would then be called out, and would also be defeated. It was not intended that the movement should appear to be of large dimensions, but that, gradually increasing in magnitude, it should, as it opened, strike terror into the heart of the slave States by the amount of organization it would exhibit, and the strength it gathered. They anticipated, after the first blow had been struck, that, by the aid of the freed and Canadian negroes who would join them, they could inspire confidence in the slaves, and induce them to rally. No intention was expressed of gathering a large body of slaves, and removing them to Canada. On the contrary, Kagi clearly stated, in answer to my inquiries, that the design was to make the fight in the mountains of Virginia, extending it to North Carolina and Tennessee, and also to the swamps of South Carolina, if possible. Their purpose was not the expatriation of one or a thousand slaves, but their liberation in the States wherein they were born, and were held in bondage. "The mountains and the swamps of the South were intended by the Almighty," said John Brown to me afterwards, "for a refuge for the slave, and a defense against the oppressor."

Kagi spoke of having marked out a chain of counties extending continuously through South Carolina, Georgia, Alabama, and Mississippi. He had traveled over a large portion of the region indicated, and from his own personal knowledge, and with the assistance of the Canadian negroes who had escaped from those States, they had arranged a general plan of attack. The counties he named were those which contained the largest proportion of slaves, and would, therefore, be the best in which to strike. The blow struck at Harper's Ferry was to be in the spring, when the planters were busy, and the slaves most needed. The arms in the arsenal were to be taken to the mountains, with such slaves as joined. The telegraph wires were to be cut and railroad tracks torn up in all directions. As fast as possible, other bands besides the original one were to be formed, and a continuous chain of posts established in the mountains. They were to be supported by provisions taken from the farms of the oppressors. They expected to be speedily and constantly reinforced; first, by the arrival of those men, who in Canada, were anxiously looking and praying for the time of deliverance, and then by the slaves themselves. The intention was to hold the egress to the free States as long as possible, in order to retreat when that was advisable. Kagi, however, expected to retreat southward, not in the contrary direction. The slaves were to be armed with pikes, scythes, muskets, shot-guns, and other simple instruments of defense; the officers, white or black, and such of the men as were skilled and trustworthy, to have the use of the Sharpe's rifles and revolvers. They anticipated procuring provisions enough for subsistence by forage, as also arms, horses, and ammunition. Kagi said one of the reasons that induced him to go into the enterprise was a full conviction that at no very distant day forcible efforts for freedom would break out among the slaves, and that slavery might be more speedily abolished by such efforts than by any other means. He knew by observation in the South, that in no point was the system so vulnerable as in its fear of a slave rising. Believing that such a blow would be soon struck, he wanted to organize it so as to make it more effectual, and also, by directing and controlling the negroes, to prevent some of the atrocities that would necessarily arise from the sudden upheaving of such a mass as the Southern slaves. The constitution adopted at Chatham was intended as the framework of organization among the emancipationists, to enable the leaders to effect a more complete control of their forces. Ignorant men, in fact, all men, were more easily managed by the forms of law and organization than without them. This was one of the purposes to be subserved by the Provisional Government. Another was to alarm the (slave-holding) oligarchy by discipline and the show of organization. In their terror they would imagine the whole North was upon them pell-mell, as well as all their slaves. Kagi said John Brown anticipated that by a system of forbearance to non-slaveholders many of them might be induced to join them.

In answer to an inquiry, Kagi stated that no politician, in the

Republican or any other party, knew of their plans, and but few of the Abolitionists. It was no use talking, he said, of anti-slavery action to non-resistant agitators. That there were men who knew John Brown's general idea is most true; but, south of the Canadian Provinces and of North Elba, there were but few who were cognizant of the mode by which he intended to mould those ideas into deeds.

After a long conversation, the substance of which I have given, we returned to the house. I had some further conversation with Brown, mostly upon his movements, and the use of arms. An allusion to the terror inspired by the fear of slaves rising, was the fact that Nat Turner with fifty men held a portion of Virginia for several weeks. The same number well organized and armed, can shake the system out of the State. . . .

FREDERICK DOUGLASS'S ACCOUNT OF HIS LAST MEETING WITH JOHN BROWN, AUGUST 19–21, 1859 [2]

His face wore an anxious expression, and he was much worn by thought and exposure. I felt that I was on a dangerous mission, and was as little desirous of discovery as himself, though no reward had been offered for me.

We—Mr. Kagi, Captain Brown, Shields Green, and myself, sat down among the rocks and talked over the enterprise which was about to be undertaken. The taking of Harper's Ferry, of which Captain Brown had merely hinted before, was now declared as his settled purpose, and he wanted to know what I thought of it. I at once opposed the measure with all the arguments at my command. To me, such a measure would be fatal to running off slaves (as was the original plan), and fatal to all engaged in doing so. It would be an attack upon the federal government, and would array the whole country against us. Captain Brown did most of the talking on the other side of the question. He did not at all object to rousing the nation; it seemed to him that something startling was just what the nation needed. He had completely renounced his old plan, and thought that the capture of Harper's Ferry would serve as notice to the slaves that their friends had come, and as a trumpet to rally them to his standard. He described the place as to its means of defense, and how impossible it would be

² From Frederick Douglass, *Life and Times of Frederick Douglass* (Hartford, Conn.: Park Publishing Co., 1881), pp. 323–25.

to dislodge him if once in possession. Of course I was no match for him in such matters, but I told him, and these were my words, that all his arguments, and all his descriptions of the place, convinced me that he was going into a perfect steel-trap, and that once in he would never get out alive; that he would be surrounded at once and escape would be impossible. He was not to be shaken by anything I could say, but treated my views respectfully, replying that even if surrounded he would find means for cutting his way out; but that would not be forced upon him; he should have a number of the best citizens of the neighborhood as his prisoners at the start, and that holding them as hostages, he should be able if worse came to worse, to dictate terms of egress from the town. I looked at him with some astonishment, that he could rest upon a reed so weak and broken, and told him that Virginia would blow him and his hostages sky-high, rather than that he should hold Harper's Ferry an hour. Our talk was long and earnest; we spent the most of Saturday and a part of Sunday in this debate—Brown for Harper's Ferry, and I against it; he for striking a blow which should instantly rouse the country, and I for the policy of gradually and unaccountably drawing off the slaves to the mountains, as at first suggested and proposed by him. When I found that he had fully made up his mind and could not be dissuaded, I turned to Shields Green and told him he heard what Captain Brown had said; his old plan was changed, and that I should return home, and if he wished to go with me he could do so. Captain Brown urged us both to go with him, but I could not do so, and could but feel that he was about to rivet the fetters more firmly than ever on the limbs of the enslaved. In parting he put his arms around me in a manner more than friendly, and said: "Come with me, Douglass, I will defend you with my life. I want you for a special purpose. When I strike the bees will begin to swarm, and I shall want you to help hive them." But my discretion or my cowardice made me proof against the dear old man's eloquence—perhaps it was something of both which determined my course. When about to leave I asked Green what he had decided to do, and was surprised by his coolly saying in his broken way, "I b'leve I'll go wid de ole man." Here we separated; they to go to Harper's Ferry, I to Rochester. There has been some difference of opinion as to the propriety of my course in thus leaving my friend. Some have thought that I ought to have gone with him, but I have no reproaches for myself at this point, and

since I have been assailed only by colored men who kept even
farther from this brave and heroic man than I did, I shall not
trouble myself much about their criticisms. They compliment
me in assuming that I should perform greater deeds than themselves. . . .

7
The War Begins

Harper's Ferry rests where the Shenandoah and Potomac rivers come together, about sixty miles from the nation's capital. Because the climate and terrain precluded extensive tobacco or cotton cultivation, there were no large plantations in the region. The population of the entire six-county surrounding area included 115,000 whites, almost 10,-000 freed Negroes, and only 18,000 slaves, many of whom were women and children.

After his final conversations with his supporters in Boston, Brown set about rounding up the recruits—mostly fugitive slaves residing in Canada—whom he expected would join his volunteer army. He then set out for the Harper's Ferry region and from his station at the Kennedy farmhouse wrote letters to John Jr. instructing him to send on the volunteers. Hardly any came. In late September, the 950 pikes which he had purchased from Charles Blair of Connecticut arrived, and in the next two weeks a few late recruits joined the party. Although John Kagi's draft plan for The Provisional Army called for a brigade of over 4,500 men (divided into four regiments, sixteen battalions, and sixty-four companies), Brown started off with only twenty-one followers (sixteen whites and five blacks), less than a third of a company.[1] He obviously intended to add liberated slaves to his volunteer army until it achieved brigade level; organizationally, if in no other way, Brown was prepared for success.

Finally, Brown decided to strike. At eight o'clock Sunday night, October 16, he left for Harper's Ferry with eighteen of his men, leaving three behind to move the supplies to another location where they could arm the slaves and others who would surely join the fight. Brown's band met no resistance entering the town and quickly secured the United States

[1] Brown's band was made up of idealistic young men devoted to the anti-slavery cause. They ranged in age from twenty to forty-nine, but the majority of them were in their twenties at the time of the raid. Twelve had been with Brown at some stage of his Kansas work; the others had met him in Canada, Ohio, Iowa, and New York during Brown's travels in 1857–1859.

armory and arsenal and seized a rifle works. Brown next sent out some of his men to round up hostages from nearby farms and to spread the news to the slaves that their liberation was at hand. A while later, Brown's men stopped a Baltimore-bound train entering Harper's Ferry, only to let it pass through and allow the trainmen to alert others to what was going on. By Monday morning Harper's Ferry was filled, not with slaves come to join the insurrection, but with armed farmers and angry militiamen come to suppress it.

F. B. SANBORN TO T. W. HIGGINSON, JUNE 4, 1859 [2]

Brown has set out on his expedition, having got some $800 from all sources except from Mr. Stearns, and from him the balance of $2000; Mr. Stearns being a man who "having put his hand to the plough turneth not back." B. left Boston for Springfield and New York on Wednesday morning at 8½ and Mr. Stearns has probably gone to N. Y. today to make final arrangements for him. He means to be on the ground as soon as he can—perhaps so as to begin by the 4th July. He could not say where he shall be for a few weeks—but a letter addressed to him under cover to his son John Jr. West Andover, Ashtabula Co. Ohio [would reach him]. This point is not far from where B. will begin, and his son will communicate with him. Two of his sons will go with him. He is desirous of getting someone to go to Canada and collect recruits for him among the fugitives, with H. Tubman, or alone, as the case may be, & urged me to go,—but my school will not let me. Last year he engaged some persons & heard of others, but he does not want to lose time by going there himself now. I suggested you to him. . . . Now is the time to help in the movement, if ever, for within the next two months the experiment will be made.

J. H. KAGI TO JOHN BROWN, JR., OCTOBER 10, 1859 [3]

Your father was here yesterday but had not time to write before returning. I shall leave here this afternoon "for good." This is the last of our stay here, for we have not $5 left, and the men must be given work or they will find it themselves. We shall not be able to receive *any thing* from you after to-day. It will not do for

[2] From Oswald Garrison Villard, *John Brown, 1800–1859: A Biography Fifty Years After* (Boston: Houghton, Mifflin, and Company, 1910), p. 396.
[3] Ibid., pp. 422–23.

any one to try to find us now. You must by all means keep back the men you talked of sending and furnish them work to live upon until you receive further instructions. Any one arriving here after to-day and trying to join us, would be trying a very hazardous and foolish experiment. They must keep off the border until we open the way clear up to the line (M. & D.'s) from the South. Until then, it will be just as dangerous here as on the other side, in fact more so: for, *there* there will be protection also, but not here. It will not do to write to Harper's Ferry. It will never get there—would do no good if it did. *You* can communicate with us thus—— (This must be a profound secret) Be sure no one gets into trouble in trying to get to us. We will try to communicate with you as soon as possible after we strike, but it may not be possible for us to do so soon. If we succeed in getting news from outside our own district it will be quite satisfactory, but we have not the most distant hope that it will be possible for us to receive *recruits* for *weeks,* or quite likely *months* to come. We must first make a complete and undisputably open road to the free states. That will require both labor and time.

This is just the right time. The year's crops have been good, and they are now perfectly housed, and in the best condition for use. The moon is just right. Slaves are discontented at this season more than at any other, the reasons for which reflection will show you. We can't live longer without money,—we couldn't get along much longer without being exposed. A great religious revival is going on, and has its advantages. Under its influence, people who are commonly barely *unfavorable* to Slavery under religious excitement in meetings speak boldly against it. In addition to this and as a stimulant to the religious feeling, a fine slave man near our headquarters, hung himself a few days ago because his master sold his wife away from him. This also arouses the slaves. There are more reasons which I could give, but I have not time. . . .

A PORTION OF JOHN COOK'S "CONFESSION," NOVEMBER, 1859 [4]

There were some six or seven in our party who did not know anything of our constitution, and, as I have since understood, were also ignorant of the plan of operations, until the Sunday morning previous to the attack. Among this number were Edwin Coppoc,

[4] From Richard J. Hinton, *John Brown and His Men* (New York: Funk & Wagnalls Company, 1894), p. 708.

Barclay Coppoc, Francis J. Merriam, Shields Green, John Copeland, and Leary.

The constitution was read to them by A. D. Stevens, and the oath afterwards administered by Captain Brown. Sunday evening, previous to our departure, Captain Brown made his final arrangements for the capture of Harper's Ferry, and gave to his men their orders. In closing, he said:—

"And now, gentlemen, let me press this one thing on your minds. You all know how dear life is to you, and how dear your lives are to your friends; and, in remembering that, consider that the lives of others are as dear to them as yours are to you; do not, therefore, take the life of any one if you can possibly avoid it, but if it is necessary to take life in order to save your own, then make sure work of it."

JOHN E. P. DAINGERFIELD'S ACCOUNT OF THE RAID [5]

> *Daingerfield was a clerk in the armory and was taken prisoner in the early morning of October 17. This is an abridgement of his narrative, which first appeared in* Century Magazine, *June 1885.*

I walked towards my office, then just within the armory inclosure, and not more than a hundred yards from my house. As I proceeded, I saw a man come out of an alley, then another and another, all coming towards me. I inquired what all this meant; they said, "Nothing, only they had taken possession of the Government works." I told them they talked like crazy men. They answered, "Not so crazy as you think, as you will soon see." Up to this time I had not seen any arms. Presently, however, the men threw back the short cloaks they wore, and disclosed Sharp's rifles, pistols, and knives. Seeing these, and fearing something serious was going on, I told the men I believed I would return home. They at once cocked their guns, and told me I was a prisoner. This surprised me, but I could do nothing, being unarmed. I talked with them some little time longer, and again essayed to go home; but one of the men stepped before me, presented his gun, and told me if I moved I would be shot down. I then asked what they intended to do with

[5] From Franklin B. Sanborn, *The Life and Letters of John Brown* (Boston: Roberts Brothers, 1891), pp. 556–60.

me. They said I was in no personal danger; they only wanted to carry me to their captain, John Smith. I asked them where Captain Smith was. They answered at the guard house, inside of the armory inclosure. I told them I would go there; that was the point for which I first started. (My office was there, and I felt uneasy lest the vault had been broken open.)

Upon reaching the gate, I saw what indeed looked like war,— negroes armed with pikes, and sentinels with muskets all around. I was turned over to "Captain Smith," who called me by name, and asked if I knew Colonel Washington and others, mentioning familiar names. I said I did; and he then said, "Sir, you will find them there," motioning me towards the engine-room. We were not kept closely confined, but were allowed to converse with him. I asked him what his object was. He replied, "To free the negroes of Virginia." He added that he was prepared to do it, and by twelve o'clock would have fifteen hundred men with him, ready armed. Up to this time the citizens had hardly begun to move about, and knew nothing of the raid. When they learned what was going on, some came out with old shotguns, and were themselves shot by concealed men. All the stores, as well as the arsenal, were in the hands of Brown's men, and it was impossible to get either arms or ammunition, there being hardly any private weapons. At last, however, a few arms were obtained, and a body of citizens crossed the river and advanced from the Maryland side. They made a vigorous attack, and in a few minutes caused all the invaders who were not killed to retreat to Brown inside of the armory gate. Then he entered the engine-house, carrying his prisoners along, or rather part of them, for he made selections. After getting into the engine-house, he made this speech: "Gentlemen, perhaps you wonder why I have selected you from the others. It is because I believe you to be more influential; and I have only to say now, that you will have to share precisely the same fate that your friends extend to my men." He began at once to bar the doors and windows, and to cut portholes through the brick wall.

Then commenced a terrible firing from without, at every point from which the windows could be seen, and in a few minutes every window was shattered, and hundreds of balls came through the doors. These shots were answered from within whenever the attacking party could be seen. This was kept up most of the day, and, strange to say, not a prisoner was hurt, though thousands of balls were imbedded in the walls, and holes shot in the doors almost large enough for a man to creep through. At night the firing ceased, for we were in total darkness, and nothing could be seen in the engine-house. During the day and night I talked much with Brown. I found him as brave as a man could be, and sensible upon all subjects except slavery. He believed it was his duty to free the slaves, even if in doing so he lost his own life. During a sharp fight one of Brown's sons was killed. He fell; then trying to raise himself, he said, "It is all over with me," and died instantly. Brown did not leave his post at the porthole; but when the fighting was over he walked to his son's body, straightened out his limbs, took off his trappings, and then, turning to me, said, "This is the third son I have lost in this cause." Another son had been shot in the morning, and was then dying, having been brought in from the street. Often during the affair in the engine-house, when his men would want to fire upon some one who might be seen passing, Brown would stop them, saying, "Don't shoot; that man is unarmed." The firing was kept up by our men all day and until late at night, and during that time several of his men were killed, but none of the prisoners were hurt, though in great danger. During the day and night many propositions, *pro* and *con*, were made, looking to Brown's surrender and the release of the prisoners, but without result.

When Colonel Lee came with the Government troops in the night, he at once sent a flag of truce by his aid, J. E. B. Stuart, to notify Brown of his arrival, and in the name of the United States to demand his surrender, advising him to throw himself on the clemency of the Government. Brown declined to accept Colonel Lee's terms, and determined to await the attack. When Stuart was admitted and a light brought, he exclaimed, "Why, aren't you old Osawatomie Brown of Kansas, whom I once had there as my prisoner?" "Yes," was the answer, "but you did not keep me." This was the first intimation we had of Brown's real name. When Colonel Lee advised Brown to trust to the clemency of the Government, Brown responded that he knew what that meant,—a rope for his men and himself; adding, "I prefer to die just here." Stuart told him he would return at early morning for his final reply, and left him. When he had gone, Brown at once proceeded to barricade the doors, windows, etc., endeavoring to make the place as strong as possible. All this time no one of Brown's men showed the slightest fear, but calmly awaited the attack, selecting the best situations to fire from, and arranging their guns and pistols so that a fresh one could be taken up as soon as one was discharged. During the night

I had a long talk with Brown, and told him that he and his men were committing treason against the State and the United States. Two of his men, hearing the conversation, said to their leader, "Are we committing treason against our country by being here?" Brown answered, "Certainly." Both said, "If that is so, we don't want to fight any more; we thought we came to liberate the slaves, and did not know that was committing treason." Both of these men were afterwards killed in the attack on the engine-house. When Lieutenant Stuart came in the morning for the final reply to the demand to surrender, I got up and went to Brown's side to hear his answer. Stuart asked, "Are you ready to surrender, and trust to the mercy of the Government?" Brown answered, "No, I prefer to die here." His manner did not betray the least alarm. Stuart stepped aside and made a signal for the attack, which was instantly begun with sledge-hammers to break down the door. Finding it would not yield, the soldiers seized a long ladder for a battering-ram, and commenced beating the door with that, the party within firing incessantly. I had assisted in the barricading, fixing the fastenings so that I could remove them on the first effort to get in. But I was not at the door when the battering began, and could not get to the fastenings till the ladder was used. I then quickly removed the fastenings; and, after two or three strokes of the ladder, the engine rolled partially back, making a small aperture, through which Lieutenant Green of the marines forced his way, jumped on top of the engine, and stood a second, amidst a shower of balls, looking for John Brown. When he saw Brown he sprang about twelve feet at him, giving an under thrust of his sword, striking Brown about midway the body, and raising him completely from the ground. Brown fell forward, with his head between his knees, while Green struck him several times over the head, and, as I then supposed, split his skull at every stroke. I was not two feet from Brown at that time. Of course I got out of the building as soon as possible, and did not know till some time later that Brown was not killed. It seems that Green's sword, in making the thrust, struck Brown's belt and did not penetrate the body. The sword was bent double. The reason that Brown was not killed when struck on the head was, that Green was holding his sword in the middle, striking with the hilt, and making only scalp wounds.

When Governor Wise came and was examining Brown, I heard the questions and answers, and no lawyer could have used more careful reserve, while at the same time he showed no disrespect.

Governor Wise was astonished at the answers he received from Brown. After some controversy between the United States and the State of Virginia, as to which had jurisdiction over the prisoners, Brown was carried to the Charlestown jail, and after a fair trial was hanged. Of course I was a witness at the trial; and I must say that I have never seen any man display more courage and fortitude than John Brown showed under the trying circumstances in which he was placed. I could not go to see him hanged. He had made me a prisoner, but had spared my life and that of other gentlemen in his power; and when his sons were shot down beside him, almost any other man similarly placed would at least have exacted life for life.

STATEMENTS BY BROWN DURING AND IMMEDIATELY AFTER THE RAID [6]

To the Master of the Armory, Whom He Held Captive

We are Abolitionists from the North, come to take and release your slaves; our organization is large, and must succeed. I suffered much in Kansas, and expect to suffer here, in the cause of human freedom. Slaveholders I regard as robbers and murderers; and I have sworn to abolish slavery and liberate my fellow-men.

To Major Russell, First Virginia Soldier to Enter the Engine House

My name is John Brown; I have been well known as Old Brown of Kansas. Two of my sons were killed here to-day, and I'm dying too. I came here to liberate slaves, and was to receive no reward. I have acted from a sense of duty, and am content to await my fate; but I think the crowd have treated me badly. I am an old man. Yesterday I could have killed whom I chose; but I had no desire to kill any person, and would not have killed a man had they not tried to kill me and my men. I could have sacked and burned the town, but did not; I have treated the persons whom I took as hostages kindly, and I appeal to them for the truth of what I say. If I had succeeded in running off slaves this time, I could have raised twenty times as many men as I have now, for a similar expedition. But I have failed.

[6] Sanborn, *John Brown*, pp. 560–61.

To a Newspaper Reporter

A lenient feeling towards the citizens led me into a parley with them as to compromise; and by prevarication on their part I was delayed until attacked, and then in self-defence was forced to intrench myself.

8

"A Conversation with Brown"

Governor Henry A. Wise and Senator James M. Mason of Virginia, Representative Clement Vallandigham of Ohio, and several newspaper reporters arrived in Harper's Ferry on Tuesday afternoon, October 18. Senator Mason led the questioning of Brown, which lasted nearly three hours, after which Wise announced that Brown "is the gamest man I ever saw." Indeed, Brown, conscious that his words were being recorded for a wider audience, sought to place his act in historical perspective and to strike a heroic pose before his examiners. Both themes would later be amplified in his prison correspondence.[1]

"Old Brown," or "Ossawatomie Brown," as he is often called, the hero of a dozen flights or so with the "border ruffians" of Missouri, in the days of "bleeding Kansas," is the head and front of this offending—the commander of the filibuster army. His wounds, which at first were supposed to be mortal, turn out to be mere flesh-wounds and scratches, not dangerous in their character. He has been removed, together with Stephens, the other wounded prisoner, from the engine-room to the office of the Armory, and they now lie on the floor, upon miserable shake-downs, covered with some old bedding.

Brown is fifty-five years of age, rather small-sized, with keen and restless grey eyes, and a grizzly beard and hair. He is a wiry, active man, and, should the slightest chance for an escape be afforded, there is no doubt that he will yet give his captors much trouble. His hair is matted and tangled, and his face, hands, and clothes, all smouched and smeared with blood. Colonel Lee stated that he would exclude all visitors from the room if the wounded men were

---

[1] From *The Life, Trial, and Execution of John Brown* (New York: Robert W. DeWitt, 1859), pp. 44–49. This book is not attributed to any author; it consists almost wholly of a newspaper correspondent's transcription of the events surrounding Brown's raid, capture, trial, and execution.

annoyed or pained by them, but Brown said he was by no means annoyed; on the contrary, he was glad to be able to make himself and his motives clearly understood. He converses freely, fluently and cheerfully, without the slightest manifestation of fear or uneasiness, evidently weighing well his words, and possessing a good command of language. His manner is courteous and affable, and he appears to make a favorable impression upon his auditory, which, during most of the day yesterday, averaged about ten or a dozen men.

When I arrived in the Armory, shortly after two o'clock in the afternoon, Brown was answering questions put to him by Senator Mason, who had just arrived from his residence at Winchester, thirty miles distant, Col. Faulkner, member of Congress, who lives but a few miles off, Mr. Vallandigham, member of Congress of Ohio, and several other distinguished gentlemen. The following is a *verbatim* report of the conversation:

Mr. Mason: Can you tell us, at least who furnished money for your expedition?

Mr. Brown: I furnished most of it myself. I cannot implicate others. It is by my own folly that I have been taken. I could easily have saved myself from it had I exercised my own better judgment, rather than yielded to my feelings.

Mr. Mason: You mean if you had escaped immediately?

Mr. Brown: No; I had the means to make myself secure without any escape, but I allowed myself to be surrounded by a force by being too tardy.

Mr. Mason: Tardy in getting away?

Mr. Brown: I should have gone away, but I had thirty odd prisoners, whose wives and daughters were in tears for their safety, and I felt for them. Besides, I wanted to allay the fears of those who believed we came here to burn and kill. For this reason I allowed the train to cross the bridge, and gave them full liberty to pass on. I did it only to spare the feelings of those passengers and their families, and to allay the apprehensions that you had got here in your vicinity a band of men who had no regard for life and property, nor any feeling of humanity.

Mr. Mason: But you killed some people passing along the streets quietly.

Mr. Brown: Well, sir, if there was anything of that kind done, it was without my knowledge. Your own citizens, who were my prisoners, will tell you that every possible means were taken to prevent it. I did not allow my men to fire, nor even to return a fire, when there was danger of killing those we regarded as innocent persons, if I could help it. They will tell you that we allowed ourselves to be fired at repeatedly and did not return it.

A Bystander: That is not so. You killed an unarmed man at the corner of the house over there [at the water tank] and another besides.

Mr. Brown: See here, my friend, it is useless to dispute or contradict the report of your own neighbors who were my prisoners.

Mr. Mason: If you would tell us who sent you here—who provided the means—that would be information of some value.

Mr. Brown: I will answer freely and faithfully about what concerns myself—I will answer anything I can with honor, but not about others.

Mr. Vallandigham (member of Congress from Ohio, who had just entered): Mr. Brown, who sent you here?

Mr. Brown: No man sent me here; it was my own prompting and that of my Maker, or that of the devil, whichever you please to ascribe it to. I acknowledge no man in human form.

Mr. Vallandigham: Did you get up the expedition yourself?

Mr. Brown: I did.

Mr. Vallandigham: Did you get up this document that is called a constitution?

Mr. Brown: I did. They are a constitution and ordinances of my own contriving and getting up.

Mr. Vallandigham: How long have you been engaged in this business?

Mr. Brown: From the breaking of the difficulties in Kansas. Four of my sons had gone there to settle, and they induced me to go. I did not go there to settle, but because of the difficulties.

Mr. Mason: How many are engaged with you in this movement? I ask those questions for our own safety.

Mr. Brown: Any questions that I can honorably answer I will, not otherwise. So far as I am myself concerned I have told everything truthfully. I value my word, sir.

Mr. Mason: What was your object in coming?

Mr. Brown: We came to free the slaves, and only that.

A Young Man (in the uniform of a volunteer company): How many men in all had you?

Mr. Brown: I came to Virginia with eighteen men only, besides myself.

Volunteer: What in the world did you suppose you could do here in Virginia with that amount of men?

Mr. Brown: Young man, I don't wish to discuss that question here.

Volunteer: You could not do anything.

Mr. Brown: Well, perhaps your ideas and mine on military subjects would differ materially.

Mr. Mason: How do you justify your acts?

Mr. Brown: I think, my friend, you are guilty of a great wrong against God and humanity—I say it without wishing to be offensive—and it would be perfectly right in any one to interfere with you so far as to free those you wilfully and wickedly hold in bondage. I do not say this insultingly.

Mr. Mason: I understand that.

Mr. Brown: I think I did right, and that others will do right who interfere with you at any time and all times. I hold that the golden rule, "Do unto others as you would that others should do unto you," applies to all who would help others to gain their liberty.

Lieut. Stuart: But you don't believe in the Bible.

Mr. Brown: Certainly I do.

Mr. Vallandigham: Where did your men come from? Did some of them come from Ohio?

Mr. Brown: Some of them.

Mr. Vallandigham: From the Western Reserve? None came from Southern Ohio?

Mr. Brown: Yes, I believe one came from below Steubenville, down not far from Wheeling.

Mr. Vallandigham: Have you been in Ohio this summer?

Mr. Brown: Yes, sir.

Mr. Vallandigham: How lately?

Mr. Brown: I passed through to Pittsburg on my way in June.

Mr. Vallandigham: Were you at any county or State fair there?

Mr. Brown: I was not—not since June.

Mr. Mason: Did you consider this a military organization, in this paper [the Constitution]? I have not yet read it.

Mr. Brown: I did in some sense. I wish you would give that paper close attention.

Mr. Mason: You considered yourself the Commander-in-Chief of these "provisional" military forces.

Mr. Brown: I was chosen agreeably to the ordinance of a certain document, commander-in-chief of that force.

Mr. Mason: What wages did you offer?

Mr. Brown: None.

Lieut. Stuart: "The wages of sin is death."

Mr. Brown: I would not have made such a remark to you, if you had been a prisoner and wounded in my hands. . . .

Mr. Vallandigham: Have you been in Portage County lately?

Mr. Brown: I was there in June last.

Mr. Vallandigham: When in Cleveland, did you attend the Fugitive Slave Law Convention there?

Mr. Brown: No. I was there about the time of the sitting of the court to try the Oberlin rescuers. I spoke there publicly on that subject. I spoke on the Fugitive Slave Law and my own rescue. Of course, so far as I had any influence at all, I was disposed to justify the Oberlin people for rescuing the slave, because I have myself forcibly taken slaves from bondage. I was concerned in taking eleven slaves from Missouri to Canada last winter. I think I spoke in Cleveland before the Convention. I do not know that I had any conversation with any of the Oberlin rescuers. I was sick part of the time I was in Ohio, with the ague. I was part of the time in Ashtabula County.

Mr. Vallandigham: Did you see anything of Joshua R. Giddings there?

Mr. Brown: I did meet him.

Mr. Vallandigham: Did you converse with him?

Mr. Brown: I did. I would not tell you, of course, anything that would implicate Mr. Giddings; but I certainly met with him and had conversations with him.

Mr. Vallandigham: About that rescue case?

Mr. Brown: Yes, I did; I heard him express his opinions upon it very freely and frankly.

Mr. Vallandigham: Justifying it?

Mr. Brown: Yes, sir; I do not compromise him certainly in saying that.

A Bystander: Did you go out to Kansas under the auspices of the Emigrant Aid Society?

Mr. Brown: No, sir; I went out under the auspices of John Brown and nobody else.

Mr. Vallandigham: Will you answer this: Did you talk with Giddings about your expedition here?

Mr. Brown: No, I won't answer that; because a denial of it I would not make, and to make any affirmation of it I should be a great dunce.

Mr. Vallandigham: Have you had any correspondence with parties at the North on the subject of this movement?

Mr. Brown: I have had correspondence.

A Bystander: Do you consider this a religious movement?

Mr. Brown: It is, in my opinion, the greatest service a man can render to God.

Bystander: Do you consider yourself an instrument in the hands of Providence?

Mr. Brown: I do.

Bystander: Upon what principle do you justify your acts?

Mr. Brown: Upon the golden rule. I pity the poor in bondage that have none to help them; that is why I am here; not to gratify any personal animosity, revenge or vindictive spirit. It is my sympathy with the oppressed and the wronged, that are as good as you and as precious in the sight of God.

Bystander: Certainly. But why take the slaves against their will?

Mr. Brown: I never did.

Bystander: You did in one instance, at least.

Stephens, the other wounded prisoner, here said, in a firm, clear voice—"You are right. In one case, I know the negro wanted to go back."

A Bystander: Where did you come from?

Mr. Stephens: I lived in Ashtabula county, Ohio.

Mr. Vallandigham: How recently did you leave Ashtabula county?

Mr. Stephens: Some months ago. I never resided there any length of time; have been through there.

Mr. Vallandigham: How far did you live from Jefferson?

Mr. Brown: Be cautious, Stephens, about any answers that would commit any friend. I would not answer that.

Stephens turned partially over with a groan of pain, and was silent.

Mr. Vallandigham (to Mr. Brown): Who are your advisers in this movement?

Mr. Brown: I cannot answer that. I have numerous sympathizers throughout the entire North.

Mr. Vallandigham: In northern Ohio?

Mr. Brown: No more there than anywhere else; in all the free States.

Mr. Vallandigham: But you are not personally acquainted in southern Ohio?

Mr. Brown: Not very much.

Mr. Vallandigham (to Stephens): Were you at the Convention last June?

Stephens: I was.

Mr. Vallandigham (to Brown): You made a speech there?

Mr. Brown: I did.

A Bystander: Did you ever live in Washington City?

Mr. Brown: I did not. I want you to understand, gentlemen—[and, to the reporter of the "Herald"] you may report that—I want you to understand that I respect the rights of the poorest and weakest of colored people, oppressed by the slave system, just as much as I do those of the most wealthy and powerful. That is the idea that has moved me, and that alone. We expect no reward, except the satisfaction of endeavoring to do for those in distress and greatly oppressed, as we would be done by. The cry of distress of the oppressed is my reason, and the only thing that prompted me to come here.

A Bystander: Why did you do it secretly?

Mr. Brown: Because I thought that necessary to success; no other reason.

Bystander: And you think that honorable? Have you read Gerritt Smith's last letter?

Mr. Brown: What letter do you mean?

Bystander: The "New York Herald" of yesterday, in speaking of this affair, mentions a letter in this way:—"Apropos of this exciting news, we recollect a very significant passage in one of Gerrit Smith's letters, published a month or two ago, in which he speaks of the folly of attempting to strike the shackles off the slaves by the force of moral suasion or legal agitation, and predicts that the next movement made in the direction of negro emancipation would be an insurrection in the South."

Mr. Brown: I have not seen the "New York Herald" for some days past; but I presume, from your remark about the gist of the letter, that I should concur with it. I agree with Mr. Smith that moral suasion is hopeless. I don't think the people of the slave States will ever consider the subject of slavery in its true light till some other argument is resorted to than moral suasion.

Mr. Vallandigham: Did you expect a general rising of the slaves in case of your success?

Mr. Brown: No, sir; nor did I wish it. I expected to gather them up from time to time and set them free.

Mr. Vallandigham: Did you expect to hold possession here till then?

Mr. Brown: Well, probably I had quite a different idea. I do not know that I ought to reveal my plans. I am here a prisoner and wounded, because I foolishly allowed myself to be so. You overrate your strength in supposing I could have been taken if I had not allowed it. I was too tardy after commencing the open attack—in delaying my movements through Monday night, and up to the time I was attacked by the government troops. It was all occasioned by my desire to spare the feelings of my prisoners and their families and the community at large. I had no knowledge of the shooting of the negro [Hayward].

Mr. Vallandigham: What time did you commence your organization in Canada?

Mr. Brown: That occurred about two years ago, if I remember right. It was, I think, in 1858.

Mr. Vallandigham: Who was the Secretary?

Mr. Brown: That I would not tell if I recollected, but I do not recollect. I think the officers were elected in May, 1858. I may answer incorrectly, but not intentionally. My head is a little confused by wounds, and my memory obscure on dates, etc.

Dr. Biggs: Were you in the party at Dr. Kennedy's house?

Mr. Brown: I was at the head of that party. I occupied the house to mature my plans. I have not been in Baltimore to purchase caps.

Dr. Biggs: What was the number of men at Kennedy's?

Mr. Brown: I decline to answer that.

Dr. Biggs: Who lanced that woman's neck on the hill?

Mr. Brown: I did. I have sometimes practised in surgery when I thought it a matter of humanity and necessity, and there was no one else to do it, but have not studied surgery.

Dr. Biggs: It was done very well and scientifically. They have been very clever to the neighbors, I have been told, and we had no reason to suspect them except that we could not understand their movements. They were represented as eight or nine persons; on Friday there were thirteen.

Mr. Brown: There were more than that.

Q.: Where did you get arms to obtain possession of the Armory?

A.: I bought them.

Q.: In what State?

A.: That I would not state.

Q.: How many guns?

A.: Two hundred Sharpe's rifles and two hundred revolvers— what is called the Massachusetts Arms Company's revolvers, a little under the navy size.

Q.: Why did you not take that swivel you left in the house?

A.: I had no occasion for it. It was given to me a year or two ago.

Q.: In Kansas?

A.: No; I had nothing given me in Kansas.

Q.: By whom; and in what State?

A.: I decline to answer. It is not properly a swivel; it is a very large rifle with a pivot. The ball is larger than a musket ball; it is intended for a slug.

Reporter of the Herald: I do not wish to annoy you; but if you have anything further you would like to say I will report it.

Mr. Brown: I have nothing to say, only that I claim to be here in carrying out a measure I believe perfectly justifiable, and not to act the part of an incendiary or ruffian, but to aid those suffering great wrong. I wish to say, furthermore, that you had better—all you people at the South—prepare yourselves for a settlement of that question that must come up for settlement sooner than you are prepared for. The sooner you are prepared the better. You may dispose of me very easily; I am nearly disposed of now; but this question is still to be settled—this negro question I mean—the end of that is not yet. These wounds were inflicted upon me—both sabre cuts on my head and bayonet stabs in different parts of my body—some minutes after I had ceased fighting and had consented to a surrender, for the benefit of others, not for my own. [This statement was vehemently denied by all around.] I believe the major [meaning Lieut. J. B. Stuart, of the United States cavalry], would not have been alive; I could have killed him just as easy as a mosquito when he came in, but I supposed he came in only to receive our surrender. There had been loud and long calls of "surrender" from us—as loud as men could yell—but in the confusion and excitement I suppose we were not heard. I do not think the major, or any one, meant to butcher us after we had surrendered.

An Officer here stated that the order to the marines were not to shoot anybody; but when they were fired upon by Brown's men and one of them killed, they were obliged to return the compliment.

Mr. Brown insisted that the marines fired first.

An Officer: Why did not you surrender before the attack?

Mr. Brown: I did not think it was my duty or interest to do so. We assured the prisoners that we did not wish to harm them, and they should be set at liberty. I exercised my best judgment, not believing the people would wantonly sacrifice their own fellow-citizens, when we offered to let them go on condition of being allowed to change our position about a quarter of a mile. The prisoners agreed by vote among themselves to pass across the bridge with us. We wanted them only as a sort of guaranty of our own safety; that we should not be fired into. We took them in the first place as hostages and to keep them from doing any harm. We did kill some men in defending ourselves, but I saw no one fire except directly in self-defense. Our orders were strict not to harm any one not in arms against us.

Q.: Brown, suppose you had every nigger in the United States, what would you do with them?

A.: Set them free.

Q.: Your intention was to carry them off and free them?

A.: Not at all.

A Bystander: To set them free would sacrifice the life of every man in this community.

Mr. Brown: I do not think so.

Bystander: I know it. I think you are fanatical.

Mr. Brown: And I think you are fanatical. "Whom the gods would destroy they first make mad," and you are mad.

Q.: Was it your only object to free the negroes?

A.: Absolutely our only object.

Q.: But you demanded and took Col. Washington's silver and watch?

A.: Yes; *we intended freely to appropriate the property of slave-holders to carry out our object.* It was for that, and only that, and with no design to enrich ourselves with any plunder whatever.

Q.: Did you know Sherrod in Kansas? I understand you killed him.

A.: I killed no man except in fair fight; I fought at Black Jack Point and Ossawatomie, and if I killed anybody it was at one of those places.

9
The Trial

Governor *Wise ordered Brown and the other raiders to stand trial in a Virginia court, even though the attack had been on federal property. Wise argued that a federal prosecution would take too long and, given the excitement generated by the raid, and the various threats to lynch its leader, Brown's life was in danger. Undoubtedly Wise also thought his opportunity for decisively handling the Brown affair would enhance his own political career. Because a grand jury was already in session in nearby Charlestown, the trial commenced on October 27 after a doctor pronounced Brown fit to appear in court. Brown, who was tried separately, was charged with murdering four whites and a Negro, with conspiring with slaves to rebel, and with treason against Virginia.*

From the start, Brown saw in his trial the chance to make his cause and purposes known to the nation. In a letter to Judge Thomas B. Russell of Boston, who was seeking counsel for the old man, Brown noted that without proper legal representation, "neither the facts of our case can come before the world nor can we have the benefit of such facts as might be considered mitigating in the view of others upon our trial." "Do not," he prudently warned, "send an ultra Abolitionist."

The haste of the trial, the inadequacy of well-prepared counsel, Brown's weakened physical condition, the decision to try him in a state court for a federal crime, and the nature of the indictment itself all provided grounds for those who wished to challenge the fairness of the trial. Brown himself spoke to this issue on the third day: "I discover that, not withstanding all the assurances I have received of a fair trial, nothing like a fair trial is to be given me, as it would seem."

On October 31, Hiram Griswold of Cleveland, the last in a succession of lawyers assigned to Brown, concluded the defense by arguing that Brown could not be guilty of treason against a state to which he owed no loyalty, that Brown had not killed anyone himself, and that the utter failure of the raid indicated that Brown had not conspired with slaves. An-

79

*drew Hunter presented the closing argument for the prosecu-
tion; after a forty-five minute deliberation, the jury found
Brown guilty on all three counts. Judge Richard Parker later
sentenced him to hang on December 2.*

*Brown rarely spoke during the six-day trial (in fact, he ap-
peared to sleep on occasion), and the selections below represent most of what he said in his own defense. His five-minute
peroration at the conclusion of the trial circulated widely in
the North and did much to present Brown as a martyr to the
cause of liberty and justice.*

"THE VIRGINIA JUDICIARY"—EDITORIAL IN
THE *NEW YORK TIMES*, OCTOBER 24, 1859

We are very glad to see, if we may judge from the charge to
the Grand Jury, which is to find the bill against Brown and his
confederates, that the Virginian judiciary are likely to do justice to
themselves and the State in dealing with the Harper's Ferry "insurrection." Nothing could be clearer, calmer, wiser, and more impartial, than the terms in which the duty of those who are charged with
the administration of the law in this unfortunate affair has been
laid down; nothing could be more patriotic than the manner in
which the supremacy of the law itself, over all popular passions and
prejudices, has been asserted. Whatever disgrace Brown's *emeute*
and the panic which it has inspired may reflect upon Virginia (and
Gov. Wise thinks it serious), she derives nothing but credit from
the attitude so far taken by the Bench. If this spirit be maintained
throughout the trial, she may almost thank the terrible Abolitionists for giving her a chance of proving to the world that she still
can show the surest indication of strength and greatness—the ability
to give her bitterest foe a fair trial in open court, without fear or
favor, on a charge of having aimed a blow at her very existence.

We know of no better test of the civilization and soundness of a
State than the tone of her judges and Bar, in dealing with a case of
this kind in a time of great popular excitement. If *they* cling to the
law and the Constitution, and hold the scales of justice with a steady
hand, it matters little how mobs may rave or riot. The world will
always take it for granted that a community which produces judges,
who preserve their composure, their honor, in the midst of tumul-
tuous passions, is sound at the core, and has still a great future in
store for it. . . .

BROWN SPEAKS AT HIS TRIAL

The first selection is taken from testimony on the second day of the trial. The second statement consists of Brown's final remarks to the court.[1]

Brown was brought in walking, and laid down on his cot at full length within the bar. He looked considerably better, the swelling having left his eyes.

Senator Mason was present.

Messrs. Harding and Hunter again appeared for the Commonwealth, and Messrs. Botts and Green for the prisoner.

Mr. Botts read the following dispatch, which was received this morning:

Akron, Ohio, Thursday, *Oct.* 26, 1859.

To C. J. Faulkner, and Lawson Botts:

John Brown, leader of the insurrection at Harper's Ferry, and several of his family have resided in this county many years. Insanity is hereditary in that family. His mother's sister died with it, and a daughter of that sister has been two years in a Lunatic Asylum. A son and daughter of his mother's brother have also been confined in the lunatic asylum, and another son of that brother is now insane and under close restraint. These facts can be conclusively proven by witnesses residing here, who will doubtless attend the trial if desired.

A. H. Lewis.

William C. Allen, telegraphic operator at the Akron office, adds to the above dispatch that A. H. Lewis is a resident of that place, and his statements are entitled to implicit credit.

Mr. Botts said that on receiving the above dispatch he went to the jail with his associate, Mr. Green, and read it to Brown, and is desired by the latter to say that in his father's family there has never been any insanity at all. On his mother's side there have been repeated instances of it. He adds that his first wife showed symptoms of it, which were also evident in his first and second sons by that

[1] From *The Life, Trial, and Execution of John Brown* (New York: Robert W. DeWitt, 1859), pp. 64–65, 94–95.

wife. Some portions of the statements in the dispatch he knows to be correct, and of other portions he is ignorant. He does not know whether his mother's sister died in the lunatic asylum, but he does believe that a daughter of that sister has been two years in the asylum. He also believes that a son and daughter of his mother's brother have been confined in an asylum; but he is not apprised of the fact that another son of that brother is now insane and in close confinement. Brown also desires his counsel to say that he does not put in the plea of insanity, and if he has been at all insane he is totally unconscious of it, yet he adds that those who are most insane generally suppose that they have more reason and sanity than those around them. For himself he disdains to put in that plea, and seeks no immunity of the kind. This movement is made totally without his approbation or concurrence, and was unknown to him, till the receipt of the dispatch above.

Brown then raised himself up in bed, and said: "I will add, if the Court will allow me, that I look upon it as a miserable artifice and pretext of those who ought to take a different course in regard to me, if they took any at all, and I view it with contempt more than otherwise. As I remarked to Mr. Green, insane persons, so far as my experience goes, have but little ability to judge of their own sanity; and, if I am insane, of course I should think I know more than all the rest of the world. But I do not think so. I am perfectly unconscious of insanity, and I reject, so far as I am capable, any attempt to interfere in my behalf on that score." . . .

[After the jury found the prisoner guilty as charged,] the clerk then asked Mr. Brown whether he had anything to say why sentence should not be pronounced upon him.

Mr. Brown immediately rose, and in a clear, distinct voice, said: "I have, may it please the Court, a few words to say. In the first place, I deny everything but what I have all along admitted, of a design on my part to free slaves. I intended certainly to have made a clean thing of that matter, as I did last winter when I went into Missouri, and there took slaves without the snapping of a gun on either side, moving them through the country, and finally leaving them in Canada. I designed to have done the same thing again on a larger scale. That was all I intended to do. I never did intend murder or treason, or the destruction of property, or to excite or incite the slaves to rebellion, or to make insurrection. I have another objection, and that is that it is unjust that I should suffer such a penalty. Had I interfered in the manner which I admit, and which I admit has been fairly proved—for I admire the truthfulness and candor of the greater portion of the witnesses who have testified in this case—had I so interfered in behalf of the rich, the powerful, the intelligent, the so-called great, or in behalf of any of their friends, either father, mother, brother, sister, wife, or children, or any of that class, and suffered and sacrificed what I have in this interference, it would have been all right, and every man in this Court would have deemed it an act worthy of reward rather than punishment. This Court acknowledges, too, as I suppose, the validity of the law of God. I see a book kissed, which I suppose to be the Bible, or at least the New Testament, which teaches me that all things whatsoever I would that men should do to me, I should do even so to them. It teaches me further to remember them that are in bonds as bound with them. I endeavored to act up to that instruction. I say I am yet too young to understand that God is any respecter of persons. I believe that to have interfered as I have done, as I have always freely admitted I have done in behalf of His despised poor, is no wrong, but right. Now, if it is deemed necessary that I should forfeit my life for the furtherance of the ends of justice, and mingle my blood further with the blood of my children and with the blood of millions in this slave country whose rights are disregarded by wicked, cruel, and unjust enactments, I say let it be done. Let me say one word further. I feel entirely satisfied with the treatment I have received on my trial. Considering all the circumstances, it has been more generous than I expected. But I feel no consciousness of guilt. I have stated from the first what was my intention, and what was not. I never had any design against the liberty of any person, nor any disposition to commit treason or excite slaves to rebel or make any general insurrection. I never encouraged any man to do so, but always discouraged any idea of that kind. Let me say also in regard to the statements made by some of those who were connected with me, I fear it has been stated by some of them that I have induced them to join me, but the contrary is true. I do not say this to injure them, but as regretting their weakness. Not one but joined me of his own accord, and the greater part at their own expense. A number of them I never saw, and never had a word of conversation with till the day they came to me, and that was for the purpose I have stated. Now, I am done."

While Mr. Brown was speaking, perfect quiet prevailed, and when he had finished the Judge proceeded to pronounce sentence upon him. After a few primary remarks, he said, that no reasonable doubt could exist of the guilt of the prisoner, and sentenced him to be hung in public, on Friday, the 2d of December next.

Mr. Brown received his sentence with composure. . . .

10

"Is He Insane?"

The question of Brown's mental balance has been central to students of Brown and the Harper's Ferry raid. The sanity question, a ploy the old man quickly rejected, was first raised formally by attorney Lawson Botts during the trial. The question next appeared after Brown's sentencing when George Hoyt, a young lawyer who had assisted in the defense, traveled to Ohio to collect affidavits regarding Brown's insanity from nineteen of his friends and relatives. Missouri Republican Montgomery Blair, for one, encouraged Hoyt's mission in hopes that by declaring Brown insane, the sectional storm touched off by the raid could be quieted.

Hoyt and others hoped that Governor Wise would seize on the possibility of declaring Brown insane and thereby deny him the divisive symbolic importance that Brown and certain northern sympathizers wanted. Wise was aware that hanging Brown might amplify his message through martyrdom, but he rejected both the insanity plea and the martyrdom question. In response to a letter from New York Mayor Fernando Wood, Wise wrote: "From honest patriotic men like yourself, many of them, I am warned that hanging will make him a martyr. Ah!—Will it?—The obvious answer to that question shows me above anything else the necessity of hanging him."

DEPOSITION OF EDWIN WETMORE, NOVEMBER 11, 1859 [1]

Personally appeared before me a notary public in and for the County of Summit aforesaid Edwin Wetmore of Stow township in said County who being duly sworn on his oath says that he has been acquainted with John Brown (now under sentence of death in Virginia) since early childhood [and] that he always regarded him as strictly honest and upright in all his dealings and of a gentle and

[1] From the Henry A. Wise Papers in the Library of Congress, Washington, D.C.

mild disposition. This was said affiants opinion of him until about a year ago when he had a conversation with him in Akron in said County of Summit, where he gave this affiant an account of the death of his sons in Kansas and also gave him what purported to be a history of his adventure there. From his statements then and the whole manner and appearance of the man he regarded him as demented and actually insane. His whole character seemed changed. [H]e appeared fanatic and furious and incapable of reasoning or of listening to reason and this affiant then stated and still believes that he was insane upon the subject of slavery and that he was a mono-maniac.

DEPOSITION OF E. N. SILL, NOVEMBER 14, 1859 [2]

I have had some acquaintance with John Brown who is now under sentence of death in the State of Virginia with his Father, a most excellent but very peculiar man I was well acquainted for many years. I have also known several of his Brothers well—All of these men have possessed more than ordinary character, and several of them very striking idiosyncrasies. John Brown, who had removed to Kansas with his family as [illegible word] for a permanent residence, returned to this vicinity, soon after the commencement there of the difficulties between the free state men & other parties and telling me the story of the wrongs of himself & family & free state friends, asked my aid to purchase arms for their defense. He said not one word of any acts of retaliation in Kansas, Missouri or elsewhere; nothing of any plan or design to liberate slaves, but only of *defense*. And in this matter I fully sympathized with him, and was more than willing to *give* the desired aid; But from his peculiarities I thought Mr. Brown an unsafe man to be commissioned with such a matter, and I neither then, nor at any other time, contributed any thing to him or through him, for this or any other purpose. I admire Mr. Brown's courage and devotion to his beliefs. But I have no confidence in the sanity of his judgement in matters appertaining to slavery. I have no doubt that, upon this subject, more especially upon *his relation* to the abolition of slavery, he is surely a monomaniac as any inmate of any lunatic asylum in the country.

² Ibid.

DEPOSITION OF DAVID L. KING, NOVEMBER 15, 1859[3]

I, David L. King of the town of Akron County of Summit & State Ohio being [illegible word] duly sworn, depose and say that I have been slightly acquainted with John Brown for from five to eight years and have considered him as lacking a "balance wheel"— about the 1st of April last having some business with a son of said Brown on a farm about 4 miles distant from this village—on my return I was requested to take said John Brown & two of his Kansas followers in my wagon to town—on the way I passed the time in conversation with Mr Brown & became convinced that on the subject of slavery he was crazy—he was armed to the teeth & remarked among other things that he was an "instrument in the hands of God to free the slaves"—I asked his followers if they were relatives of Mr Brown—they said no that they were all "Sons of Liberty" & were on there way to Kansas to engage in the good work & that they always went armed & would never be taken alive—

PORTION OF AN INTERVIEW WITH MRS. JOHN BROWN[4]

Is he Insane?

I then put the question which I had been chiefly solicitious to ask, "It is the common talk of the newspapers that Capt. Brown is insane; what do you say to that opinion?"

"I never knew," she replied "of his insanity, until I read it in the newspapers. He is a clear-headed man. He has always been, and now is, entirely in his right mind. He is always cool, deliberate, and never over-hasty; but he has always considered that his first perceptions of duty, and his first impulses to action, were the best, and the safest to be followed. He has almost always acted upon his first suggestions. No, he is not insane. His reason is clear. His last act was the result, as all others have been, of his truest and strongest conscientious convictions."

[3] Ibid.
[4] From The *New York Times*, November 18, 1859.

11

"I Am Permitted to Die For a Cause"

The Virginia authorities allowed Brown to receive visitors and correspond with family and acquaintances during his stay in jail. The moving and self-assured quality of his last letters contributed much to his canonization as an abolitionist martyr. Characteristic of Brown's correspondence throughout his life, these letters mingle his intense concern with practical family affairs with his reflections on the meaning of his life's central mission.

Missing from this correspondence are any letters to supporters which might implicate them in the raid. Indeed, such implications had already appeared in the satchel of papers— including maps with southern towns marked and incriminating letters from his northern backers—which Brown had left at the Kennedy farmhouse. The publication of these documents by The New York Times and The New York Herald sent a shock of horror through the ranks of Brown's financial backers. Gerrit Smith became hysterical, fearing that he would be captured and put to death, and on November 7 had himself confined to an insane asylum. When summoned to testify before the Senate committee investigating the raid, Sanborn fled to Canada. Howe and Stearns had earlier sought refuge in Canada as well, from where Howe issued a statement to The New York Tribune disassociating himself from the invasion. With Parker already in Europe, Higginson alone stood his ground and refused to flee or burn his correspondence with Brown, as others had done. In November, a conspirator to the last, Higginson worked on an elaborate plan to rescue Brown and seize the incriminating documents, but the scheme was dropped when Brown announced that he wanted no part of it and was quite prepared to hang.

Brown and his men received many visitors in jail, some coming to express sympathy, others to castigate them. On December 1 his wife joined him for his last meal. When the jailer denied her permission to stay for the night, Brown lost *his composure for the first and only time. Quickly recovering, he returned to his cell to spend a restless last night on earth. Brown arose at dawn on December 2, read his Bible, and wrote a last letter to Mary, enclosing his will and giving instructions for the inscriptions on the old family monument at North Elba. At eleven o'clock, after handing a note to one of his guards, Brown was escorted through a crowd of nearly 2,000 soldiers and spectators who had gathered to watch the execution. "This is a beautiful country," he remarked as the wagon took him to the gallows, "I never had the pleasure of seeing it before."*

BROWN TO HIS FAMILY, OCTOBER 31, 1859 [1]

My dear Wife and Children, every one,

I suppose you have learned before this by the newspapers that two weeks ago today we were fighting for our lives at Harper's Ferry; that during the fight Watson was mortally wounded, Oliver killed, William Thompson killed, and Dauphin slightly wounded; that on the following day I was taken prisoner, immediately after which I received several sabre-cuts on my head and bayonet-stabs in my body. As nearly as I can learn, Watson died of his wound on Wednesday, the second—or on Thursday, the third—day after I was taken. Dauphin was killed when I was taken, and Anderson I suppose also. I have since been tried, and found guilty of treason, etc., and of murder in the first degree. I have not yet received my sentence. No others of the company with whom you were acquainted were, so far as I can learn, either killed or taken. Under all these terrible calamities, I feel quite cheerful in the assurance that God reigns and will overrule all for his glory and the best possible good. I feel no consciousness of guilt in the matter, nor even mortification on account of my imprisonment and irons; and I feel perfectly sure that very soon no member of my family will feel any possible disposition to "blush on my account." Already dear friends at a distance, with kindest sympathy, are cheering me with the assurance that posterity, at least, will do me justice. I shall commend you all together, with my beloved but bereaved daughters-in-law, to their sympathies, which I do not doubt will soon reach you. I also commend you all to Him "whose mercy endureth forever,"—to the God of my fathers, "whose

[1] From Franklin B. Sanborn, *The Life and Letters of John Brown* (Boston: Roberts Brothers, 1891), pp. 579–80.

I am, and whom I serve." "He will never leave you nor forsake you," unless you forsake Him. Finally, my dearly beloved, be of good comfort. Be sure to remember and follow my advice, and my example too, so far as it has been consistent with the holy religion of Jesus Christ,—in which I remain a most firm and humble believer. Never forget the poor, nor think anything you bestow on them to be lost to you, even though they may be black as Ebedmelech, the Ethiopian eunuch, who cared for Jeremiah in the pit of the dungeon; or as black as the one to whom Philip preached Christ. Be sure to entertain strangers, for thereby some have—"Remember them that are in bonds as bound with them."

I am in charge of a jailer like the one who took charge of Paul and Silas; and you may rest assured that both kind hearts and kind faces are more or less about me, while thousands are thirsting for my blood. "These light afflictions, which are but for a moment, shall work out for us a far more exceeding and eternal weight of glory." I hope to be able to write you again. Copy this, Ruth, and send it to your sorrow-stricken brothers to comfort them. Write me a few words in regard to the welfare of all. God Almighty bless you all, and make you "joyful in the midst of all your tribulations!" Write to John Brown, Charleston, Jefferson County, Va., care of Captain John Avis.

BROWN TO "E. B.," NOVEMBER 1, 1859 [2]

Your most cheering letter of the 27th of October is received; and may the Lord reward you a thousandfold for the kind feeling you express toward me; but more especially for your fidelity to the "poor that cry, and those that have no help." For this I am a prisoner in bonds. It is solely my own fault, in a military point of view, that we met with our disaster. I mean that I mingled with our prisoners and so far sympathized with them and their families that I neglected my duty in other respects. But God's will, not mine, be done.

You know that Christ once armed Peter. So also in my case I think he put a sword into my hand, and there continued it so long as he saw best, and then kindly took it from me. I mean when I first went to Kansas. I wish you could know with what cheerfulness I am now wielding the "sword of the Spirit" on the right hand and on the left. I bless God that it proves "mighty to the pulling down of strongholds." I always loved my Quaker friends, and I commend

[2] Ibid., pp. 582–83.

to their kind regard my poor bereaved widowed wife and my daughters and daughters-in-law, whose husbands fell at my side. One is a mother and the other likely to become so soon. They, as well as my own sorrow-stricken daughters, are left very poor, and have much greater need of sympathy than I, who, through Infinite Grace and the kindness of strangers, am "joyful in all my tribulations."

Dear sister, write them at North Elba, Essex County, N.Y., to comfort their sad hearts. Direct to Mary A. Brown, wife of John Brown. There is also another—a widow, wife of Thompson, who fell with my poor boys in the affair at Harper's Ferry—at the same place.

I do not feel conscious of guilt in taking up arms; and had it been in behalf of the rich and powerful, the intelligent, the great (as men count greatness), or those who form enactments to suit themselves and corrupt others, or some of their friends, that I interfered, suffered, sacrificed, and fell, it would have been doing very well. But enough of this. These light afflictions, which endure for a moment, shall but work for me "a far more exceeding and eternal weight of glory." I would be very grateful for another letter from you. My wounds are healing. Farewell. God will surely attend to his own cause in the best possible way and time, and he will not forget the work of his own hands.

BROWN TO HIS FAMILY, NOVEMBER 8, 1859 [3]

Dear Wife and Children, every one,

I will begin by saying that I have in some degree recovered from my wounds, but that I am quite weak in my back and sore about my left kidney. My appetite has been quite good for most of the time since I was hurt. I am supplied with almost everything I could desire to make me comfortable, and the little I do lack (some articles of clothing which I lost) I may perhaps soon get again. I am, besides, quite cheerful, having (as I trust) "the peace of God, which passeth all understanding," to "rule in my heart," and the testimony (in some degree) of a good conscience that I have not lived altogether in vain. I can trust God with both the time and the manner of my death, believing, as I now do, that for me at this time to seal my testimony for God and humanity with my blood will do vastly more toward advancing the cause I have earnestly endeavored to promote,

³ Ibid., pp. 585–87.

than all I have done in my life before. I beg of you all meekly and quietly to submit to this, not feeling yourselves in the least *degraded* on that account. Remember, dear wife and children all, that Jesus of Nazareth suffered a most excruciating death on the cross as a felon, under the most aggravating circumstances. Think also of the prophets and apostles and Christians of former days, who went through greater tribulations than you or I, and try to be reconciled. May God Almightly comfort all your hearts, and soon wipe away all tears from your eyes! To him be endless praise! Think, too, of the crushed millions who "have no comforter." I charge you all never in your trials to forget the griefs "of the poor that cry, and of those that have none to help them." I wrote most earnestly to my dear and afflicted wife not to come on for the present, at any rate. I will now give her my reasons for doing so. First, it would use up all the scanty means she has, or is at all likely to have, to make herself and children comfortable hereafter. For let me tell you that the sympathy that is now aroused in your behalf may not always follow you. There is but little more of the romantic about helping poor widows and their children than there is about trying to relieve poor "niggers." Again, the little comfort it might afford us to meet again would be dearly bought by the pains of a final separation. We must part; and I feel assured for us to meet under such dreadful circumstances would only add to our distress. If she comes on here, she must be only a gazing-stock throughout the whole journey, to be re-marked upon in every look, word, and action, and by all sorts of creatures, and by all sorts of papers, throughout the whole country. Again, it is my most decided judgment that in quietly and submissively staying at home vastly more of generous sympathy will reach her, without such dreadful sacrifice of feeling as she must put up with if she comes on. The visits of one or two female friends that have come on here have produced great excitement, which is very annoying; and they cannot possibly do me any good. Oh, Mary! do not come, but patiently wait for the meeting of those who love God and their fellow-men, where no separation must follow. "They shall go no more out forever." I greatly long to hear from some one of you, and to learn anything that in any way affects your welfare. I sent you ten dollars the other day; did you get it? I have also endeavored to stir up Christian friends to visit and write to you in your deep affliction. I have no doubt that some of them, at least, will heed the call. Write to me, care of Captain John Avis, Charlestown, Jefferson County, Virginia.

"Finally, my beloved, be of good comfort." May all your names be "written in the Lamb's book of life!"—may you all have the purifying and sustaining influence of the Christian religion! . . .

P.S. I cannot remember a night so dark as to have hindered the coming day, nor a storm so furious or dreadful as to prevent the return of warm sunshine and a cloudless sky. But, beloved ones, do remember that this is not your rest,—that in this world you have no abiding place or continuing city. To God and his infinite mercy I always commend you.

BROWN TO REVEREND H. L. VAILL, NOVEMBER 15, 1859 [4]

Your most kind and most welcome letter of the 8th inst. reached me in due time. I am very grateful for all the good feeling you express, and also for the kind counsels you give, together with your prayers in my behalf. Allow me here to say, notwithstanding "my soul is among lions," still I believe that "God in very deed is with me." You will not, therefore, feel surprised when I tell you that I am "joyful in all my tribulations"; that I do not feel condemned of Him whose judgment is just, nor of my own conscience. Nor do I feel degraded by my imprisonment, my chains, or prospect of the gallows. I have not only been (though utterly unworthy) permitted to "suffer affliction with God's people," but have also had a great many rare opportunities for "preaching righteousness in the great congregation." I trust it will not all be lost. The jailer (in whose charge I am) and his family and assistants have all been most kind; and notwithstanding he was one of the bravest of all who fought me, he is now being abused for his humanity. So far as my observation goes, none but brave men are likely to be humane to a fallen foe. "Cowards prove their courage by their ferocity." It may be done in that way with but little risk.

I wish I could write you about a few only of the interesting times I here experience with different classes of men, clergymen among others. Christ, the great captain of liberty as well as of salvation, and who began his mission, as foretold of him, by proclaiming it, saw fit to take from me a sword of steel after I had carried it for a time; but he has put another in my hand ("the sword of the Spirit"), and I pray God to make me a faithful soldier, wherever he may send me, not less on the scaffold than when surrounded by my warmest sympathizers.

[4] Ibid., pp. 589–91.

My dear old friend, I do assure you I have not forgotten our last meeting, nor our retrospective look over the route by which God had then led us; and I bless his name that he has again enabled me to hear your words of cheering and comfort at a time when I, at least, am on the "brink of Jordan." (See Bunyan's "Pilgrim.") God in infinite mercy grant us soon another meeting on the opposite shore. I have often passed under the rod of him whom I call my Father,—and certainly no son ever needed it oftener; and yet I have enjoyed much of life, as I was enabled to discover the secret of this somewhat early. It has been in making the prosperity and happiness of others my own; so that really I have had a great deal of prosperity. I am very prosperous still; and looking forward to a time when "peace on earth and good-will to men" shall everywhere prevail, I have no murmuring thoughts or envious feelings to fret my mind. "I'll praise my Maker with my breath." . . .

As I believe most firmly that God reigns, I cannot believe that anything I have done, suffered, or may yet suffer will be lost to the cause of God or of humanity. And before I began my work at Harper's Ferry, I felt assured that in the worst event it would certainly pay. I often expressed that belief; and I can now see no possible cause to alter my mind. I am not as yet, in the main, at all disappointed. I have been a good deal disappointed as it regards myself in not keeping up to my own plans; but I now feel entirely reconciled to that, even,—for God's plan was infinitely better, no doubt, or I should have kept to my own. Had Samson kept to his determination of not telling Delilah wherein his great strength lay, he would probably have never overturned the house. I did not tell Delilah, but I was induced to act very contrary to my better judgment; and I have lost my two noble boys, and other friends, if not my two eyes.

But "God's will, not mine, be done." I feel a comfortable hope that, like that erring servant of whom I have just been writing, even I may (through infinite mercy in Christ Jesus) yet "die in faith." As to both the time and manner of my death,—I have but very little trouble on that score, and am able to be (as you exhort) "of good cheer." . . .

BROWN TO ANDREW HUNTER (PROSECUTOR AT BROWN'S TRIAL), NOVEMBER 22, 1859 [5]

I have just had my attention called to a seeming confliction between the statement I at first made to Governor Wise and that which I made at the time I received my sentence, regarding my intentions respecting the slaves we took *about the Ferry*. There need be no such confliction, and a few words of explanation will, I think, be quite sufficient. I had given Governor Wise a *full and particular* account of that, and when called in court to say whether I had anything further to urge, I was taken wholly by surprise, as I did not expect my sentence before the others. In the hurry of the moment, I forgot much that I had before *intended to say*, and did *not* consider the full bearing of what *I then said*. I intended to convey this idea, that it was my object to place the slaves in a condition to defend their liberties, if they would, *without any bloodshed, but not* that I intended *to run them out of the slave States*. I was not *aware* of any such apparent confliction until my attention *was called* to it, and I do not suppose that a man in *my then circumstances* should be *superhuman* in respect to the *exact purport* of every word he might utter. What I said to Governor Wise was spoken with all the deliberation I was master of, *and was intended for truth;* and what I said in court was *equally intended for truth,* but required a more full explanation *than I then gave*. Please make such use of this as you think calculated to correct any *wrong* impressions I may have given.

BROWN TO REVEREND MC FARLAND, NOVEMBER 23, 1859 [6]

Although you write to me as a stranger, the spirit you show towards me and the cause for which I am in bonds makes me feel towards you as a dear friend. I would be glad to have you or any of my liberty-loving ministerial friends here, to talk and pray with me. I am not a stranger to the way of salvation by Christ. From my youth I have studied much on that subject, and at one time hoped to be a minister myself; but God had another work for me to

[5] From *Report of the Select Committee of the Senate Appointed to Inquire into the Late Invasion and Seizure of the Public Property at Harper's Ferry*. Report Com. No. 278, 36th Congress, 1st Session, "Testimony" (Washington, D.C., 1860), pp. 67–68.

[6] Sanborn, *John Brown*, pp. 598–99.

do. To me it is given, in behalf of Christ, not only to believe on him, but also to suffer for his sake. But while I trust that I have some experimental and saving knowledge of religion, it would be a great pleasure to me to have some one better qualified than myself to lead my mind in prayer and meditation, now that my time is so near a close. You may wonder, are there no ministers of the gospel here? I answer, no. There are no ministers of Christ here. These ministers who profess to be Christian, and hold slaves or advocate slavery, I cannot abide them. My knees will not bend in prayer with them, while their hands are stained with the blood of souls. The subject you mention as having been preaching on the day before you wrote to me is one which I have often thought of since my imprisonment. I think I feel as happy as Paul did when he lay in prison. He knew if they killed him, it would greatly advance the cause of Christ; that was the reason he rejoiced so. On that same ground "I do rejoice, yea, and will rejoice." Let them hang me; I forgive them, and may God forgive them, for they know not what they do. I have no regret for the transaction for which I am condemned. I went against the laws of men, it is true, but "whether it be right to obey God or men, judge ye." Christ told me to remember them that were in bonds as bound with them, to do towards them as I would wish them to do towards me in similar circumstances. My conscience bade me do that. I tried to do it, but failed. Therefore I have no regret on that score. I have no sorrow either as to the result, only for my poor wife and children. They have suffered much, and it is hard to leave them uncared for. But God will be a husband to the widow and a father to the fatherless.

I have frequently been in Wooster, and if any of my old friends from about Akron are there, you can show them this letter. I have but a few more days, and I feel anxious to be away "where the wicked cease from troubling, and the weary are at rest." Farewell.

BROWN TO REVEREND DR. HEMAN HUMPHREY, NOVEMBER 25, 1859 [7]

My dear and honored Kinsman,

Your very sorrowful, kind, and faithful letter of the 20th instant is now before me. I accept it with all kindness. I have honestly endeavored to profit by the faithful advice it contains. Indeed, such advice could never come amiss. You will allow me to say that

[7] Ibid., pp. 603–605.

I deeply sympathize with you and all my sorrowing friends in their grief and terrible mortification. I feel ten times more afflicted on their account than on account of my own circumstances. But I must say that I am neither conscious of being "infatuated" nor "mad." You will doubtless agree with me in this,—that neither imprisonment, irons, nor the gallows falling to one's lot are of themselves evidence of either guilt, "infatuation, or madness."

I discover that you labor under a mistaken impression as to some important facts, which my peculiar circumstances will in all probability prevent the possibility of my removing; and I do not propose to take up any argument to prove that any motion or act of my life is right. But I will here state that I know it to be wholly my own fault as a leader that caused our disaster. Of this you have no proper means of judging, not being on the ground, or a practical soldier. I will only add, that it was in yielding to my feelings of humanity (if I ever exercised such a feeling), in leaving my proper place and mingling with my prisoners to quiet their fears, that occasioned our being caught. I firmly believe that God reigns, and that he overrules all things in the best possible manner; and in that view of the subject I try to be in some degree reconciled to my own weaknesses and follies even.

If you were here on the spot, and could be with me by day and by night, and know the facts and how my time is spent here, I think you would find much to reconcile your own mind to the ignominious death I am about to suffer, and to mitigate your sorrow. I am, to say the least, quite cheerful. "He shall begin to deliver Israel out of the hand of the Philistines." This was said of a poor erring servant many years ago; and for many years I have felt a strong impression that God had given me powers and faculties, unworthy as I was, that he intended to use for a similar purpose. This most unmerited honor He has seen fit to bestow; and whether, like the same poor frail man to whom I allude, my death may not be of vastly more value than my life is, I think quite beyond all human foresight. I really have strong hopes that notwithstanding all my many sins, I too may yet die "in faith."

If you do not believe I had a murderous intention (while I *know* I had not), why grieve so terribly on my account? The scaffold has but few terrors for me. God has often covered my head in the day of battle, and granted me many times deliverances that were almost so miraculous that I can scarce realize their truth; and now, when it seems quite certain that he intends to use me in a different way, shall I not most cheerfully go? I may be deceived, but I humbly trust that he will not forsake me "till I have showed his favor to this generation and his strength to every one that is to come." Your letter is most faithfully and kindly written, and I mean to profit by it. I am certainly quite grateful for it. I feel that a great responsibility rests upon me as regards the lives of those who have fallen and may yet fall. I must in that view cast myself on the care of Him "whose mercy endureth forever." If the cause in which I engaged in any possible degree approximated to be "infinitely better" than the one which Saul of Tarsus undertook, I have no reason to be ashamed of it; and indeed I cannot now, after more than a month for reflection, find in my heart (before God in whose presence I expect to stand within another week) any cause for shame.

I got a long and most kind letter from your pure-hearted brother Luther, to which I replied at some length. The statement that seems to be going around in the newspapers that I told Governor Wise that I came on here to seek revenge for the wrongs of either myself or my family, is utterly false. I never intended to convey such an idea, and I bless God that I am able even now to say that I have never yet harbored such a feeling. See testimony of witnesses who were with me while I had one son lying dead by my side, and another mortally wounded and dying on my other side. I do not believe that Governor Wise so understood, and I think he ought to correct that impression. The impression that we intended a general insurrection is equally untrue. . . .

BROWN TO JUDGE DANIEL R. TILDEN, NOVEMBER 28, 1859 [8]

Your most kind and comforting letter of the 23d inst. is received. I have no language to express the feelings of gratitude and obligation I am under for your kind interest in my behalf ever since my disaster. The great bulk of mankind estimate each other's actions and motives by the measure of success or otherwise that attends them through life. By that rule, I have been one of the worst and one of the best of men. I do not claim to have been one of the latter, and I leave it to an impartial tribunal to decide whether the world has been the worse or the better for my living and dying in it. My present great anxiety is to get as near in readiness for a different field of action as I well can, since being in a good measure

8 Ibid., pp. 609–10.

relieved from the fear that my poor broken-hearted wife and children would come to immediate want. May God reward a thousand-fold all the kind efforts made in their behalf! I have enjoyed remarkable cheerfulness and composure of mind ever since my confinement; and it is a great comfort to feel assured that I am permitted to die for a cause,—not merely to pay the debt of nature, as all must. I feel myself to be most unworthy of so great distinction. The particular manner of dying assigned to me gives me but very little uneasiness. I wish I had the time and the ability to give you, my dear friend, some little idea of what is daily, and I might almost say hourly, passing within my prison walls; and could my friends but witness only a few of these scenes, just as they occur, I think they would feel very well reconciled to my being here, just what I am, and just as I am. My whole life before had not afforded me one half the opportunity to plead for the right. In this, also, I find much to reconcile me to both my present condition and my immediate prospect. I may be very insane; and I am so, if insane at all. But if that be so, insanity is like a very pleasant dream to me. I am not in the least degree conscious of my ravings, of my fears, or of any terrible visions whatever; but fancy myself entirely composed, and that my sleep, in particular, is as sweet as that of a healthy, joyous little infant. I pray God that he will grant me a continuance of the same calm but delightful dream, until I come to know of those realities which eyes have not seen and which ears have not heard. I have scarce realized that I am in prison or in irons at all. I certainly think I was never more cheerful in my life. . . .

BROWN TO MRS. GEORGE L. STEARNS, NOVEMBER 29, 1859 [9]

No letter I have received since my imprisonment here has given me more satisfaction or comfort than yours of the 8th instant. I am quite cheerful, and was never more happy. Have only time to write a word. May God forever reward you and all yours! My love to all who love their neighbors. I have asked to be spared from having any weak or hypocritical prayers made over me when I am publicly murdered, and that my only religious attendants be poor little dirty, ragged, bareheaded, and barefooted slave boys and girls, led by some old gray-headed slave mother.

Farewell! Farewell!

[9] Ibid., pp. 610–11.

BROWN TO HIS FAMILY, NOVEMBER 30, 1859 [10]

My dearly beloved Wife, Sons, and Daughters, every one,

As I now begin probably what is the last letter I shall ever write to any of you, I conclude to write to all at the same time. I will mention some little matters particularly applicable to little property concerns in another place.

I recently received a letter from my wife, from near Philadelphia, dated November 22, by which it would seem that she was about giving up the idea of seeing me again. I had written her to come on if she felt equal to the undertaking, but I do not know that she will get my letter in time. It was on her own account, chiefly, that I asked her to stay back. At first I had a most strong desire to see her again, but there appeared to be very serious objections; and should we never meet in this life, I trust that she will in the end be satisfied it was for the best at least, if not most for her comfort.

I am waiting the hour of my public murder with great composure of mind and cheerfulness; feeling the strong assurance that in no other possible way could I be used to so much advantage to the cause of God and of humanity, and that nothing that either I or all my family have sacrificed or suffered will be lost. The reflection that a wise and merciful as well as just and holy God rules not only the affairs of this world but of all worlds, is a rock to set our feet upon under all circumstances,—even those more severely trying ones in which our own feelings and wrongs have placed us. I have now no doubt but that our seeming disaster will ultimately result in the most glorious success. So, my dear shattered and broken family, be of good cheer, and believe and trust in God with all your heart and with all your soul; for He doeth all things well. Do not feel ashamed on my account, nor for one moment despair of the cause or grow weary of well-doing. I bless God I never felt stronger confidence in the certain and near approach of a bright morning and glorious day than I have felt, and do now feel, since my confinement here. I am endeavoring to return, like a poor prodigal as I am, to my Father, against whom I have always sinned, in the hope that he may kindly and forgivingly meet me, though a very great way off.

Oh, my dear wife and children, would to God you could know how I have been travailing in birth for you all, that no one of you may fail of the grace of God through Jesus Christ; that no one of you may be blind to the truth and glorious light of his Word, in which life and immortality are brought to light. I beseech you, every one, to make the Bible your daily and nightly study, with a child-like, honest, candid, teachable spirit of love and respect for your husband and father. And I beseech the God of my fathers to open all your eyes to the discovery of the truth. You cannot imagine how much you may soon need the consolations of the Christian religion. Circumstances like my own for more than a month past have convinced me, beyond all doubt, of my own great need of some theories treasured up, when our prejudices are excited, our vanity worked up to the highest pitch. Oh, do not trust your eternal all upon the boisterous ocean, without even a helm or compass to aid you in steering! I do not ask of you to throw away your reason; I only ask you to make a candid, sober use of your reason.

My dear young children, will you listen to this last poor admonition of one who can only love you? Oh, be determined at once to give your whole heart to God, and let nothing shake or alter that resolution. You need have no fears of regretting it. Do not be vain and thoughtless, but sober-minded; and let me entreat you all to love the whole remnant of our once great family. Try and build up again your broken walls, and to make the utmost of every stone that is left. Nothing can so tend to make life a blessing as the consciousness that your life and example bless and leave others stronger. Still, it is ground of the utmost comfort to my mind to know that so many of you as have had the opportunity have given some proof of your fidelity to the great family of men. Be faithful unto death: from the exercise of habitual love to man it cannot be very hard to love his Maker.

I must yet insert the reason for my firm belief in the divine inspiration of the Bible, notwithstanding I am, perhaps, naturally sceptical,—certainly not credulous. I wish all to consider it most thoroughly when you read that blessed book, and see whether you cannot discover such evidence yourselves. It is the purity of heart, filling our minds as well as work and actions, which is everywhere insisted on, that distinguishes it from all the other teachings, that commends it to my conscience. Whether my heart be willing and obedient or not, the inducement that it holds out is another reason of my conviction of its truth and genuineness; but I do not here omit this my last argument on the Bible, that eternal life is what my soul is panting after this moment. I mention this as a reason for endeavoring to leave a valuable copy of the Bible, to be carefully preserved in remembrance of me, to so many of my posterity, instead of some other book at equal cost.

I beseech you all to live in habitual contentment with moderate circumstances and gains of worldly store, and earnestly to teach this to your children and children's children after you, by example as well as precept. Be determined to know by experience, as soon as may be, whether Bible instruction is of divine origin or not. Be sure to owe no man anything, but to love one another. John Rogers wrote to his children: "Abhor that arrant whore of Rome." John Brown writes to his children to abhor, with undying hatred also, that sum of all villanies,—slavery. Remember, "he that is slow to anger is better than the mighty," and "he that ruleth his spirit than he that taketh a city." Remember also that "they being wise shall shine, and they that turn many to righteousness, as the stars for ever and ever."

And now, dearly beloved family, to God and the work of his grace I commend you all.

BROWN'S LAST NOTE [11]

I John Brown am now quite *certain* that the crimes of this *guilty land: will* never be purged *away;* but with Blood. I had *as I now think: vainly* flattered myself that without *very much* bloodshed; it might be done.

THE EXECUTION OF JOHN BROWN [12]

At eleven o'clock on Friday, Dec. 2d, John Brown was brought out of the jail accompanied by Sheriff Campbell and assistants, and Capt. Avis, the jailer. . . .

Brown was a accompanied by no ministers, he desiring no religious services either in the jail or on the scaffold.

On reaching the field where the gallows was erected, the prisoner said, "Why are none but military allowed in the inclosure? I am sorry citizens have been kept out." On reaching the gallows he observed Mr. Hunter and Mayor Green standing near, to whom he said, "Gentlemen, good bye," his voice not faltering.

[11] From the John Brown Papers, Chicago Historical Society, Chicago, Illinois. Reprinted by permission.
[12] *The Life, Trial, and Execution of John Brown* (New York: Robert W. De-Witt, 1859), pp. 100–101.

The prisoner walked up the steps firmly, and was the first man on the gallows. Avis and Sheriff Campbell stood by his side, and after shaking hands, and bidding an affectionate adieu, he thanked them for their kindness. When the cap was put over his face, and the rope around his neck, Avis asked him to step forward on the trap. He replied, "You must lead me, I cannot see." The rope was adjusted, and the military order given, "Not ready yet." The soldiers marched, countermarched, and took position as if an enemy were in sight, and were thus occupied for nearly ten minutes, the prisoner standing all the time. Avis inquired if he was not tired. Brown said "No, not tired; but don't keep me waiting longer than is necessary."

While on the scaffold, Sheriff Campbell asked him if he would take a handkerchief in his hand to drop as a signal when he was ready. He replied, "No, I do not want it—but do not detain me any longer than is absolutely necessary."

He was swung off at fifteen minutes past eleven. A slight grasping of the hands and twitching of the muscles were seen, and then all was quiet.

The body was several times examined, and the pulse did not cease until thirty-five minutes had passed. The body was then cut down, placed in a coffin and conveyed under military escort to the depot, where it was put in a car to be carried to the ferry by a special train at four o'clock. . . .

PART TWO

THE RESPONSES TO JOHN BROWN AND THE HARPER'S FERRY RAID

The contemporary responses to John Brown and Harper's Ferry varied widely. Sections 12, 13, and 14 contain excerpts from the writings and speeches of those who sought to interpret and use the man and the event. In reading these selections, one not only senses the meaning of John Brown but also confronts the climate of opinion of a nation on the verge of war.

12

Martyr and Symbol

A number of northern intellectuals, clergymen, and reformers quickly set out to present Brown as an abolitionist saint, a picture which Brown himself helped create through his utterances and prison letters. Brown was aware of the proclamations being made on his behalf; when he read a newspaper account of Henry Ward Beecher's statement, "Let no man pray that Brown be spared. Let Virginia make him a martyr," Brown pencilled "Good" in the margin. The various responses to Brown were not always predictable; William Lloyd Garrison, for instance, overcame his dedication to nonviolence to praise Brown's raid. The excerpts from the speeches of Beecher, Phillips, Garrison, and Emerson exemplify the kinds of responses that confirmed the South's fears that John Brown was the vanguard of a pervasive assault on slavery.

Unlike these men, John Greenleaf Whittier deplored what he called Brown's "rash and insane attempt." Whittier, a Quaker pacifist, declined an invitation to write a memorial poem for the day of the execution and instead published "Brown of Ossawatomie" in The New York Independent on

December 22, 1859. Criticized by Brown's sympathizers as too harsh on the old man and by detractors as too favorable, this poem was among the most popular reflections on its subject in the nineteenth century.

In sharp contrast to the responses of northern sympathizers, southern spokesmen used Harper's Ferry as an occasion to intensify the fears and passions of their fellow southerners and to encourage them to combat those who, like Brown, sought to destroy their institutions and way of life. For men like George Fitzhugh (author of the proslavery book, Cannibals All!*) and Edmund Ruffin (a prominent exponent of southern nationalism), the significant and frightening meaning of Brown and his raid was their belief that they were part of an aggressive northern conspiracy against their section. Few southerners attempted to assess Brown the man; those who did saw him as a money-grubbing and besotten old man, a tool in the hands of cowardly northerners like William H. Seward and Gerrit Smith. The excerpts from the poem* The Mock Auction *offer a sample of this view.*

HENRY WARD BEECHER, "THE NATION'S DUTY TO SLAVERY," OCTOBER 30, 1859 [1]

An old man, kind at heart, industrious, peaceful, went forth, with a large family of children, to seek a new home in Kansas. That infant colony held thousands of souls as noble as liberty ever inspired or religion enriched. A great scowling Slave State, its nearest neighbor, sought to tread down this liberty-loving colony, and to dragoon slavery into it by force of arms. The armed citizens of a hostile State crossed the State lines, destroyed the freedom of the ballot-box, prevented a fair expression of public sentiment, corruptly usurped law-making power, and ordained by fraud laws as infamous as the sun ever saw; assaulted its infant settlements with armed hordes, ravaged the fields, destroyed harvests and herds, and carried death to a multitude of cabins. The United States government had no marines for this occasion! No Federal troops posted in the cars by night and day for the poor, the weak, the grossly wronged men of Kansas. There was an army there that unfurled the banner of the Union, but it was on the side of the wrong-doers, not on the side of the injured.

[1] From Henry Ward Beecher, *Patriotic Addresses* (New York: Fords, Howard, & Hulbert, 1887), pp. 206–207.

It was in this field that Brown received his impulse. A tender father, whose life was in his son's life, he saw his first-born seized like a felon, chained, driven across the country, crazed by suffering and heat, beaten like a dog by the officer in charge, and long lying at death's door! Another noble boy, without warning, without offense, unarmed, in open day, in the midst of the city, was shot dead! No justice sought out the murderers; no United States attorney was dispatched in hot haste; no marines or soldiers aided the wronged and weak!

The shot that struck the child's heart crazed the father's brain. Revolving his wrongs, and nursing his hatred of that deadly system that breeds such contempt of justice and humanity, at length his phantoms assume a slender reality, and organize such an enterprise as one might expect from a man whom grief had bereft of good judgment. He goes to the heart of a Slave State. One man,—and with sixteen followers! he seizes two thousand brave Virginians, and holds them in duress!

When a great State attacked a handful of weak colonists the government and nation were torpid, but when seventeen men attacked a sovereign State, then Maryland arms, and Virginia arms, and the United States government arms, and they three rush against seventeen men.

Travelers tell us that the Geysers of Iceland—those singular boiling springs of the North—may be transported with fury by plucking up a handful of grass or turf and throwing it into the springs. The hot springs of Virginia are of the same kind! A handful of men was thrown into them, and what a boiling there has been!

But, meanwhile, no one can fail to see that this poor, child-bereft old man is the manliest of them all. Bold, unflinching, honest, without deceit or evasion, refusing to take technical advantages of any sort, but openly avowing his principles and motives, glorying in them in danger and death, as much as when in security,—that wounded old father is the most remarkable figure in this whole drama. The Governor, the officers of the State, and all the attorneys are pygmies compared with him.

I deplore his misfortunes. I sympathize with his sorrows. I mourn the hiding or obscuration of his reason. I disapprove of his mad and feeble schemes. I shrink from the folly of the bloody foray, and I shrink likewise from all the anticipations of that judicial bloodshed, which doubtless ere long will follow,—for when was cowardice ever magnanimous? If they kill the man, it will not be so much for treason as for the disclosure of their cowardice!

Let no man pray that Brown be spared. Let Virginia make him a martyr. Now, he has only blundered. His soul was noble; his work miserable. But a cord and a gibbet would redeem all that, and round up Brown's failure with a heroic success.

WENDELL PHILLIPS, "THE LESSON OF THE HOUR," NOVEMBER 1, 1859 [2]

I said that the lesson of the hour was insurrection. I ought not to apply that word to John Brown of Osawatomie, for there was no insurrection in his case. It is a great mistake to call him an insurgent. This principle that I have endeavored so briefly to open to you, of absolute right and wrong, states what? Just this: "Commonwealth of Virginia!" There is no such thing. Lawless, brutal force is no basis of a government, in the true sense of that word. . . . No civil society, no government, can exist except on the basis of the willing submission of all its citizens, and by the performance of the duty of rendering equal justice between man and man.

Whatever calls itself a government, and refuses that duty, or has not that assent, is no government. It is only a pirate ship. Virginia, the Commonwealth of Virginia! She is only a chronic insurrection. I mean exactly what I say. I am weighing my words now. She is a pirate ship, and John Brown sails the sea a Lord High Admiral of the Almighty, with his commission to sink every pirate he meets on God's ocean of the nineteenth century. [Cheers and applause.] I mean literally and exactly what I say. In God's world there are no majorities, no minorities; one, on God's side, is a majority. You have often heard here, doubtless, and I need not tell you, the ground of morals. The rights of that one man are as sacred as those of the miscalled Commonwealth of Virginia. Virginia is only another Algiers. The barbarous horde who gag each other, imprison women for teaching children to read, prohibit the Bible, sell men on the auction-block, abolish marriage, condemn half their women to prostitution, and devote themselves to the breeding of human beings for sale, is only a larger and blacker Algiers. The only prayer of a true man for such is, "Gracious Heaven! unless they repent, send soon

<hr>

[2] From James Redpath, *Echoes of Harper's Ferry* (Boston: Thayer and Eldridge, 1860), pp. 51–52, 57–58.

their Exmouth and Decatur." John Brown has twice as much right
to hang Governor Wise, as Governor Wise has to hang him. [Cheers
and hisses.] . . .

. . . Now, the South has extensive schemes. She grasps with one
hand a Mexico, and with the other she dictates terms to the Church,
she imposes conditions on the state, she buys up Webster with a
little or a promise, and Everett with nothing. [Great laughter and
applause.] John Brown has given her something else to think of. He
has turned her attention inwardly. He has taught her that there has
been created a new element in this Northern mind; that it is not
merely the thinker, that it is not merely the editor, that it is not
merely the moral reformer, but the idea has pervaded all classes of
society. Call them madmen if you will. Hard to tell who's mad. The
world says one man is mad. John Brown said the same of the Governor. You remember the madman in Edinburgh. A friend asked
him what he was there for. "Well," cried he, "they said at home
that I was mad; and I said I was not; but they had the majority."
[Laughter.] Just so it is in regard to John Brown. The nation says
he is mad. I appeal from Philip drunk to Philip sober; I appeal
from the American people, drunk with cotton, and the New York
Observer, [loud and long laughter,] to the American people fifty
years hence, when the light of civilization has had more time to
penetrate, when self-interest has been rebuked by the world rising
and giving its verdict on these great questions, when it is not a
small band of Abolitionists, but the civilization of the twentieth
century, in all its varied forms, interests, and elements, which under-
takes to enter the arena, and discuss this last great reform. When
that day comes, what will be thought of these first martyrs, who
teach us how to live and how to die? . . .

WILLIAM LLOYD GARRISON, SPEECH ON JOHN BROWN, DECEMBER 2, 1859 [3]

As it respects his object at Harper's Ferry, it has been truly
stated here by those who have preceded me, and by John Brown
himself, whose declarations to the court have been read. The man
who brands him as a traitor is a calumniator. (Applause.) The man
who says that his object was to promote murder, or insurrection,

---

[3] From *The Liberator* (Boston), December 16, 1859.

or rebellion, is, in the language of the apostle, "a liar, and the truth is not in him." (Loud applause.) John Brown meant to effect, if possible, a peaceful exodus from Virginia; and had not his large humanity overpowered his judgment in regard to his prisoners, he would in all probability have succeeded, and not a drop of blood would have been shed. But it is asked, "Did he not have stored up a large supply of Sharp's rifles and spears? What did they mean?" Nothing offensive, nothing aggressive. Only this:—he designed getting as many slaves as he could to join him, and then putting into their hands those instruments for self-defence. But, mark you! self-defence, not in standing their ground, but on their retreat to the mountains; on their flight to Canada; not with any design or wish to shed the blood or harm the hair of a single slaveholder in the State of Virginia, if a conflict could be avoided. Remember that he had the whole town in his possession for thirty-six hours; and if he had been the man so basely represented in certain quarters, he might have consummated any thing in the way of violence and blood. But, all the while, he was counselling the strictest self-defence, and forbearance to the utmost, even when he had his enemies completely in his power. . . .

Was John Brown justified in his attempt? Yes, if Washington was in his; if Warren and Hancock were in theirs. If men are justified in striking a blow for freedom, when the question is one of a three-penny tax on tea, then, I say, they are a thousand times more justified, when it is to save fathers, mothers, wives and children from the slave-coffle and the auction block, and to restore to them their God-given rights. (Loud applause.) Was John Brown justified in interfering in behalf of the slave population of Virginia, to secure their freedom and independence? Yes, if LaFayette was justified in interfering to help our revolutionary fathers. If Kosciusko, if Pulaski, if Steuben, if De Kalb, if all who joined them from abroad were justified in that act, then John Brown was incomparably more so. If you believe in the right of assisting men to fight for freedom who are of your own color—(God knows nothing of color or complexion —human rights know nothing of these distinctions)—then you must cover, not only with a mantle of charity, but with the admiration of your hearts, the effort of John Brown at Harper's Ferry.

I am trying him by the American standard; and I hesitate not to say, with all deliberation, that those who are attempting to decry him are dangerous members of the community; they are those in whom the love of liberty has died out; they are the lineal descendants of the tories of the Revolution, only a great deal worse. (Applause.) If the spirit of '76 prevailed to-day, as it did at that period, it would make the soil of the Commonwealth too hot to hold them. (Loud applause.) . . .

A word upon the subject of Peace. I am a non-resistant—a believer in the inviolability of human life, under all circumstances; I, therefore, in the name of God, disarm John Brown, and every slave at the South. But I do not stop there; if I did, I should be a monster. I also disarm, in the name of God, every slaveholder and tyrant in the world. (Loud applause.) For wherever that principle is adopted, all fetters must instantly melt, and there can be no oppressed, and no oppressor, in the nature of things. How many agree with me in regard to the doctrine of the inviolability of human life? How many non-resistants are there here to-night? (A single voice—"I.") There is *one!* (Laughter.) Well, then, you who are otherwise are not the men to point the finger at John Brown, and cry "traitor"—judging you by your own standard. (Applause.) Nevertheless, I am a non-resistant and I not only desire, but have labored unremittingly to effect, the peaceful abolition of slavery, by an appeal to the reason and conscience of the slaveholder; yet, as a peace man—an "ultra" peace man—I am prepared to say, "Success to every slave insurrection at the South, and in every slave country." (Enthusiastic applause.) And I do not see how I compromise or stain my peace profession in making that declaration. Whenever there is a contest between the oppressed and the oppressor,—the weapons being equal between the parties,—God knows my heart must be with the oppressed, and always against the oppressor. Therefore, whenever commenced, I cannot but wish success to all slave insurrections. (Loud applause.) I thank God when men who believe in the right and duty of wielding carnal weapons are so far advanced that they will take those weapons out of the scale of despotism, and throw them into the scale of freedom. It is an indication of progress, and a positive moral growth; it is one way to get up to the sublime platform of non-resistance; and it is God's method of dealing retribution upon the head of the tyrant. Rather than see men wear their chains in a cowardly and servile spirit, I would, as an advocate of peace, much rather see them breaking the head of the tyrant with their chains. Give me, as a non-resistant, Bunker Hill, and Lexington, and Concord, rather than the cowardice and servility of a Southern slave plantation.

RALPH WALDO EMERSON, "JOHN BROWN," JANUARY 6, 1860 [4]

He grew up a religious and manly person, in severe poverty; a fair specimen of the best stock of New England; having that force of thought and that sense of right which are the warp and woof of greatness. Our farmers were Orthodox Calvinists, mighty in the Scriptures; had learned that life was a preparation, a "probation," to use their word, for a higher world, and was to be spent in loving and serving mankind.

Thus was formed a romantic character absolutely without any vulgar trait; living to ideal ends, without any mixture of self-indulgence or compromise, such as lowers the value of benevolent and thoughtful men we know; abstemious, refusing luxuries, not sourly and reproachfully but simply as unfit for his habit; quiet and gentle as a child in the house. And, as happens usually to men of romantic character, his fortunes were romantic. Walter Scott would have delighted to draw his picture and trace his adventurous career. A shepherd and herdsman, he learned the manners of animals, and knew the secret signals by which animals communicate. He made his hard bed on the mountains with them; he learned to drive his flock through thickets all but impassable; he had all the skill of a shepherd by choice of breed and by wise husbandry to obtain the best wool, and that for a course of years. And the anecdotes preserved show a far seeing skill and conduct which, in spite of adverse accidents, should secure, one year with another, an honest reward, first to the farmer, and afterwards to the dealer. If he kept sheep, it was with a royal mind; and if he traded in wool, he was a merchant prince, not in the amount of wealth, but in the protection of the interests confided to him.

I am not a little surprised at the easy effrontery with which political gentlemen, in and out of Congress, take it upon them to say that there are not a thousand men in the North who sympathize with John Brown. It would be far safer and nearer the truth to say that all people, in proportion to their sensibility and self-respect, sympathize with him. For it is impossible to see courage, and disinterestedness, and the love that casts out fear, without sympathy.

All women are drawn to him by their predominance of sentiment. All gentlemen, of course, are on his side. I do not mean by "gentle-

⁴ Redpath, *Echoes of Harper's Ferry*, pp. 120–22.

men," people of scented hair and perfumed handkerchiefs, but men of gentle blood and generosity, "fulfilled with all nobleness," who, like the Cid, give the outcast leper a share of their bed; like the dying Sidney, pass the cup of cold water to the wounded soldier who needs it more. For what is the oath of gentle blood and knighthood? What but to protect the weak and lowly against the strong oppressor?

Nothing is more absurd than to complain of this sympathy, or to complain of a party of men united in opposition to Slavery. As well complain of gravity, or the ebb of the tide. Who makes the Abolitionist? The Slaveholder. The sentiment of mercy is the natural recoil which the laws of the universe provide to protect mankind from destruction by savage passions. And our blind statesmen go up and down, with committees of vigilance and safety, hunting for the origin of this new heresy. They will need a very vigilant committee indeed to find its birthplace, and a very strong force to root it out. For the arch-Abolitionist, older than Brown, and older than the Shenandoah Mountains, is Love, whose other name is Justice, which was before Alfred, before Lycurgus, before Slavery, and will be after it.

JOHN GREENLEAF WHITTIER, "BROWN OF OSSAWATOMIE" [5]

John Brown of Ossawatomie spake on his dying day:
"I will not have to shrive my soul a priest in Slavery's pay.
But let some poor slave-mother whom I have striven to free,
With her children, from the gallows-stair put up a prayer for me!"

John Brown of Ossawatomie, they led him out to die;
And lo! a poor slave-mother with her little child pressed nigh.
Then the bold, blue eye grew tender, and the old harsh face grew
    mild,
As he stooped between the jeering ranks and kissed the negro's child!

The shadows of his stormy life that moment fell apart;
And they who blamed the bloody hand forgave the loving heart.

[5] From John Greenleaf Whittier, *The Complete Poetical Works of John Greenleaf Whittier* (Boston, 1883), p. 258. In this poem, Whittier utilized an erroneous newspaper report which described Brown kissing a slave mother's child on the way to the gallows (he in fact kissed the two-year-old son of jailer John Avis) and thereby transformed this error into an enduring legend.

That kiss from all its guilty means redeemed the good intent,
And round the grisly fighter's hair the martyr's aureole bent!

Perish with him the folly that seeks through evil good!
Long live the generous purpose unstained with human blood!
Not the raid of midnight terror, but the thought which underlies;
Not the borderer's pride of daring, but the Christian's sacrifice.

Nevermore may yon Blue Ridges the Northern rifle hear,
Nor see the light of blazing homes flash on the negro's spear.
But let the free-winged angel Truth their guarded passes scale,
To teach that right is more than might, and justice more than mail!

So vainly shall Virginia set her battle in array;
In vain her trampling squadrons knead the winter snow with clay.
She may strike the pouncing eagle, but she dares not harm the dove;
And every gate she bars to Hate shall open wide to Love!

GEORGE FITZHUGH, "DISUNION WITHIN THE UNION" [6]

The Harper's Ferry affair, with its extensive Northern ramifications, gives a new interest to the question of disunion. The most conservative must see, and if honest will admit, that the settlement of Northerners among us is fraught with danger. Not one in twenty of such settlers might tamper with our slaves and incite them to insurrection, but one man can fire a magazine, and no on can foresee where the match will be applied, or what will be the extent and consequences of the explosion. Our wives and our daughters will see in every new Yankee face an abolition missionary. We, the men of the South, may feel for their fears, and go about to remove the cause that excites them, without being amenable to the charge of cowardice or of over-cautiousness. . . .

To effect this, two measures are necessary. The one, State legislation that shall require all New-England emigrants to give security for their good behavior. The other, the renewal of the African slave-trade, to fill up that vacuum in our population which will be filled up by abolitionists if not by negroes. The Constitution of the United States stands in the way of neither measure. It is wonderfully comprehensive and elastic, and gives an adaptability and plasticity to our institutions which constitute their chief merit.

[6] From *DeBow's Review, 28* (January, 1860), 1–5, 7.

New-Englanders coming to the South, according to the most rigid construction of the common law, are *quoad ons,* persons of *ill favor,* suspicious persons (far more so than idle eaves-droppers), who may and should be required to give security for their good behavior. . . .

Each State for itself may pass laws entirely prohibiting all trade or intercourse between its citizens and the citizens of one or more of the Northern States. Each Southern State may enact that all "Yankee notions," goods, wares, and merchandise, shall be forfeited *when brought South,* as fully and completely as negro slaves are when carried *North.* White Yankees are more dangerous to our peace than English or Northern free negroes; and South Carolina has established the right to prohibit the introduction of the latter. Under the law of nations, we may, and should, exclude people whose general character is that of hostility to our institutions. It is an inalienable right, for it is the right of self-defense and self-preservation. . . .

. . . this is no dispute between Northerners and Southerners; but between conservatives and revolutionists; between Christians and infidels; between law and order men and no-government men; between the friends of private property and socialists and agrarians; between the chaste and the libidinous; between marriage and free-love; between those who believe in the past, in history, in human experience, in the Bible, in human nature, and those who, . . . foolishly, rashly, and profanely, attempt to "expel human nature," to bring about a millennium, and inaugurate a future wholly unlike anything that has preceded it. The great Christian and conservative party throughout the world is now with us. If we scorn and repudiate their alliance, if we arrogantly set up for ourselves, we thereby admit and assert that our cause and our institutions are at war with the common, moral, and religious notions of mankind. Let us rather prove to the virtuous, the religious, and conservative, that our cause is their cause, our institutions those which God has ordained, and human experience ratified and confirmed; and that to war against us, is to incite the socialists to war against everything sacred, valuable, or venerable in free society. Let us show them that every abolitionist of distinction is an agrarian, infidel, no-government man, a free-love man—more dangerous at home than to us. . . .

. . . If the South be true to herself, if she have one tittle of self-appreciation, if she can possibly be made to comprehend her own position, the post of honor is hers, and she will become the pattern, the exemplar, the leader of Christendom. She, alone, has retained that great institution, which philosophy and history, God and nature, proclaim to be necessary to man's well-being. She, alone, has made adequate provision for the laboring man. She, alone, has a contented, moral, religious society, undisturbed by infidelity, socialism, riots, revolutions, and famine. She, alone, can say to the world, we present the model which you must imitate in reforming your institutions.

EDMUND RUFFIN, "RESOLUTION OF THE CENTRAL SOUTHERN RIGHTS ASSOCIATION" [7]

The Central Southern Rights Association, first formed in Virginia in 1851, was reorganized in December, 1859.

Resolved, That the late outbreak at Harper's Ferry, of a long-concocted and wide-spread Northern conspiracy, for the destruction by armed violence and bloodshed of all that is valuable for the welfare, safety, and even existence of Virginia and the other Southern States, was, in the prompt and complete suppression of the attempt, and in all its direct results, a failure no less abortive and contemptible than the design and means employed, and objects aimed at, were malignant, atrocious, and devilish.

Resolved, That, nevertheless, the indirect results of this Northern conspiracy, and attempted deadly assault and warfare on Virginia, are all-important for the consideration and instruction of the Southern people, and especially in these respects, to wit: 1st, As proving to the world the actual condition of entire submission, obedience, and general loyalty of our negro slaves, in the fact that all the previous and scarcely impeded efforts of Northern abolitionists and their emissaries, aided by all that falsehood and deception could effect, did not operate to seduce a single negro in Virginia to rebel, or even to evince the least spirit of insubordination. 2d, As showing, in the general expression of opinion in the Northern States, through the press and from the pulpit, from prominent or leading public men, and also in the only public meetings yet held, and generally by the great popular voice of the North, that the majority, or at least the far greater number of all whose opinions have yet been expressed, either excuse, or desire to have pardoned, or sympathise with, or openly and heartily applaud the actors in this

[7] From *DeBow's Review*, 28 (March, 1860), 356.

conspiracy and attack, which could have been made successful only by the means of laying waste the South and extinguishing its institutions and their defenders by fire and sword, and with outrages more horrible than merely general massacre—while the Northern friends of the South, and of the cause of right and law, are too few, or too timid to speak openly in our support, or even to make their dissent heard, and too weak to contend with the more numerous and violent assaults of the South.

Resolved, That the time has come when every State and every man of the South should determine to act promptly and effectively for the defence of our institutions and dearest rights, as well as for other important, though less vital interests; and we earnestly appeal, especially to the legislature of Virginia, and also to the legislatures of all others of the slaveholding States, that they will hasten to consult and to deliberate, and will maturely consider and discuss the condition of the Southern States, under all past aggressions and wrongs, especially this last and crowning aggression of Northern usurpation and hatred, and devise suitable and efficient measures for the defense of the Southern people and their institutions, from the unceasing hostility and unscrupulous assaults of Northern enemies, fanatics and conspirators.

MANN SATTERWHITE VALENTINE, *THE MOCK AUCTION* [8]

In the following selections from this mock epic poem, Brown ("Ossawatomie") is portrayed consulting with Gerrit Smith ("Craven Heart") and others about his plans.

They stared into his swarthy face,
So destitute of every grace;
For he looked like unearthly creature,
With phiz of malignant nature,
With gloating eyes of Boa Constrictor,
And beak for nose, like to vulture,
Mouth of insatiate glutton
Bound with leathery tortoise-skin,
And head of bristling porcupine,

[8] From Mann Satterwhite Valentine, *The Mock Auction: Ossawatomie Sold, A Mock Heroic Poem* (Richmond, Virginia, 1860), pp. 67–69, 154–55.

Poised on neck of wiry serpentine;
His long and lathy frame—remnant
Of famine, unutterably scant,
Yet, quick spirited and brawny,
When contrasted with the flabby
Figment of softest flesh and nerve
You might, in Craven Heart observe; . . .
    The wild old Ossawatomie
Fairly embosomed with the Free,
Would drink his liquor with a vim,
And then draw the other two to him,
Saying—"My larks! we must be done
With this gibberish talking-mum;
We should be laying out our toils,—
I feel the urgent lack of spoils,
This resting on one's oars so long,
Is to my mind entirely wrong;
I, sirs! am ready primed for deeds,
To suit the cogency of needs;
I have stolen no horse for days,
I am getting rusty in my ways,—
With houses, none to fire by me,
It seems I am purging deviltry.
Here by your proffers I've been kept
Wasting the virtues of adept,
Till, presently, I will forget
The means my appetite to whet;
For blood and rapine doth require
Dexterity as well as fire;
I must do murder, if tis you;
Haste! prepare me work, or you rue
The hour you sent for such cattle,
To pitch into your slow battle;
I tell you, sirs, you have a Greek
In me! I want to hear you speak? . . .
Here at home voting other's deeds,
As safe investment for your needs.
You are a gen'rous host, I ween,
Yourselves to forego the battle scene,
Endowing me as substitute,
My family being destitute;
How great must be the exertion
Required, for this friendly diversion . . .
Wonders lie dormant in my nature,

Elements of marvellous creature,
The sledge-hammer vim of Hercules,
The dogged apathy of Diogenes,
Conjoin'd to the powers of others,
Both heroes and philosophers."

13
Editorial Reactions

The character of John Brown and the nature of the Harper's Ferry raid produced few calm and balanced responses. The editorial opinions cited in this section are indicative of the widely divergent views of the man and the act— views molded in large part by the political affiliations, sectional allegiances, and moral outlooks of the various newspapers. As these selections indicate, the several papers not only responded to Brown and the raid but also tried to locate their meanings in the wider context of contemporary issues. The sectional tension, already severe, was thereby exacerbated. Although most editorials stridently praised or denounced the old man, some, notably The New York Times, offered a more balanced and detached outlook and warned of the threat to the fragile union posed by the sensational press coverage of him and the raid.

CHICAGO PRESS AND TRIBUNE, OCTOBER 21, 1859

Who's To Blame?

A squad of fanatics whose zeal is wonderfully disproportioned to their sense, and a double-handful of slaves whose ignorance is equalled only by their desire for the freedom of which they have been robbed,—all commanded by a man who has, for years been as mad as a March hare, unite in making an insurrection at Harper's Ferry. They break into and take possession of an United States Armory, stop a railway train, kill a few citizens, assume commanding positions about the town; and for a few hours meet with none to dispute their right. They are guilty of the most incomprehensible stupidity and folly as well as unpardonable criminality in all these acts; and when their career is arrested, their leader shot down and his followers are dispersed, there is not a public journal of any party, or public man of any shade of opinion found to approve their means or justify their ends. But what matters is that the stark mad enterprise was the product of addled brains; that in itself is incontestible evidence of the insanity of its originator; that its chief in his confession claims all the credit and all the criminality for himself; that the purposes of the *emeute* are foreign to Republican policy; that the means chosen for its consummation are utterly repugnant to Republican sense of right and wrong,—in spite of these, the journals of the bogus Democracy have already begun their lying assertions that for the insurrection and its consequences the Republican party are to be held accountable! Human mendacity could go no further.

Who supposes that such an outbreak would have been possible in 1853? . . . What disturbed that era of good feeling? What stirred up the bitter waters anew? What produced that aggression in the South that gives fanaticism like that of Brown a pretext for such deeds as have just been done in Virginia? Are the Republicans responsible? Did they break up the old compact between the North and the South? Did they disregard the policy and forget the traditions of the Fathers? Did they seek out new and strange excuses why the action of the Government should be reversed, and Slavery made paramount to Freedom? Did they contrive that Dred Scott decision by which the civilized world was shocked and four millions of men were cast out of the pale of humanity? Did they renew the war, the agitation, the strife? Did they carry bloodshed to Kansas in the attempt to plant Slavery there by fire and the sword? Did they awaken the passions of hate and revenge by which the country has been torn, and by which slave insurrections with the aid of white men are made possible? Let the Democrats reply! . . .

. . . Brown is no worse, with all his crimes on his head, than Jeff. Davis. He is less a traitor to-day. His confederates have not half the criminality of many men who occupy seats in Congress or give advice in the councils of the Democratic party. But we excuse nor justify neither. We class them all together—Black Douglases and white, old Brown and Senator Brown, the insurrectionists at Harper's Ferry and the secessionists of Mississippi—all disturbers of the public peace—all howlers who care nothing for country or consequences—all traitors dyed in the wool. Brown, braver than the others, has attempted what his compeers in the South only threaten. Dissolution of the Union is the object of all.

THE *NEW YORK DAILY TRIBUNE,* OCTOBER 28, 1859

Kansas Fruits

Those who are now straining every nerve to make party capital out of Old Brown, are careful not to look back so far as to see how and why he became a monomaniac. They look away from the fact that his attempt to get up an insurrection in Virginia is a legitimate consequence of the Kansas-Nebraska bill, and, but for the passage of that measure, would never have happened. President Pierce and Judge Douglas are thus the real authors of the late insurrection. . . .

John Brown is a natural production, born on the soil of Kansas, out of the germinating heats the great contest on the soil of that Territory engendered. Before the day of Kansas outrages and oppression, no such person as Ossawatomie Brown existed. No such person could have existed. He was born of rapine, and cruelty, and murder. Revenge rocked his cradle, disciplined his arm, and nerved his soul. We do not mean to say that revenge alone was the motive-power that actuated him. His moral nature was roused, and its instincts and logic backed his determination with a profound power. But Kansas deeds, Kansas experiences, Kansas discipline, created John Brown as entirely and completely as the French Revolution created Napoleon Bonaparte. He is as much the fruit of Kansas as Washington was the fruit of our own Revolution.

Let those, then, who have reproaches to heap upon the authors of the Harper's Ferry bloody tumult and general Southern fright go back to the true cause of it all. Let them not blame blind and inevitable instruments in the work nor falsely malign those who are in no wise implicated, directly or indirectly; but let them patiently investigate the true source whence this demonstration arose, and then bestow their curses and their anathemas accordingly. It is childish and absurd for Governor Wise to seize and sit astride the wounded, panting body of Old Brown, and think he has got the villain who set this mischief on foot. By no means. The head conspirators against the peace of Virginia are ex-President Franklin Pierce and Senator Douglas. They are the parties he should apprehend, confine, and try, for causing this insurrection. Next to them, he should seize upon Senators Mason and Hunter of Virginia, as accessories. Let him follow up by apprehending every supporter of the Nebraska bill, and when he shall have brought them all to condign punishment, he will have discharged his duty, but not till then. . . .

RICHMOND DAILY ENQUIRER, NOVEMBER 2, 1859

A Suggestion for Governor Wise

Under this head, the "New York Commercial Advertiser," a Black Republican Free-soil sheet, puts forth an argument to show that Brown is an "ultra-fanatic," "little better than insane," "with mind and heart alike too warped for him to discern evil from good." Under these circumstances, the "Advertiser," argues that it would not be good *policy* for Virginia to hang Brown and his fellow-murderers. . . .

. . . A cunning policy does the "Advertiser" suggest. Pardon the *principal* and permit the *accessories* to escape! Extend clemency to Brown and forgiveness to Seward, Hale, Giddings, Smith and Greeley!—The "Advertiser" begs the Executive of Virginia not to make a martyr of Brown; that being a fanatic he is insane certainly to some degree, and our New York contemporary fears direful consequences will spring from his execution. That as the blood of the martyrs was the seed of the Church, so from the grave of John Brown the "Advertiser" fears a crop of armed fanatics may spring up destructive to Virginia and the South. It would perhaps have been more to the point to have shown that the pardon of Brown would have lessened the number of existing fanatics rather than by suggesting their increase from a due course of justice. But we apprehend the Executive of Virginia will not turn an attentive ear to suggestions coming from such a source as the New York Commercial "Advertiser." The Republican party, of which the "Advertiser" is an organ, is too deeply implicated in the actions of their chief leaders to offer suggestions with regard to the just punishment of one of their numbers. . . .

Violated laws and murdered citizens demand a victim at the hand of justice, if Brown is a crazed fanatic, irresponsible either in morals or law, there are yet guilty parties. He is then the agent of wicked principals. If the Northern people believe Brown insane, what punishment is due to those who have poisoned his mind with the "irrepressible conflict" and spurred his fanaticism to deeds of blood and carnage? He may be insane, but there are other *criminals,* guilty wretches, who instigated the crimes perpetrated at Harper's Ferry.

Bring these men, bring Seward, Greeley, Giddings, Hale and Smith to the jurisdiction of Virginia, and Brown and his deluded victims in the Charlestown jail may hope for pardon. In the opinion of Virginia the five Republican leaders, above mentioned, are more guilty than even John Brown and his associates. An ignorant fanaticism may be pleaded in paliation of the crime of Brown, but the five Republican leaders would spurn such a stultifying plea! They would not compromise their intelligence even at the cost of their morality. Let the friends of Brown, let all who believe him to be insane, and all who intend to represent him as a crazy fanatic, for whose folly no party is responsible, deliver up Seward, Greeley, Giddings, Smith and Hale. A fair trial, at their own time, with their own counsel, will be freely given them, and if Virginia does not prove them guilty, they too shall go unhurt.

SOUTHERN WATCHMAN, NOVEMBER 3, 1859 [1]

The Harper's Ferry Insurrection

This subject still engrosses much of the public attention. It has been condemned, so far as we have observed, by the Black Republican newspapers. They ought, however, to possess sufficient penetration to perceive that however far they might themselves be from engaging directly in the treasonable plots of Ossawatamie Brown, the general tone of their papers, like the sentiments of Seward's speech, has a tendency to incite other fanatics, less prudent, to the commission of acts of treason and bloodshed.

Some of the Northern papers are reading to the South lectures on the subject of the outbreak, and remind our people that they are quietly reposing on the crust of a volcano, ready at any moment to burst forth and destroy them. This, they say, is the lesson the late outbreak teaches. No fool-hardy enthusiasts ever missed the mark further. It teaches a lesson to the fanatics of the North. It shows them that the slaves their misdirected philanthropy would relieve are so well satisfied with their condition that they will not join them in their rebellion. And by the time the outraged sovereignty of Virginia has been satisfied, they will learn one other great lesson, viz: that the South can produce hemp enough to hang all the traitors the great "Northern hive" can send among her people to stir up sedition and insurrection!

[1] (Athens, Georgia)

It teaches the whole country—all sections of it—a great lesson, which we hope all will profit by—that is, that the everlasting agitation of the slavery question will inevitably lead to civil war and bloodshed! Let the people, then, of all parties—all those who would preserve the Union as our fathers made it—indignantly rebuke the agitators and drive them back to their kennels. The present is a propitious time to begin such a work. Let the people but will it, and agitation must cease. Let it go on, and the sun of liberty will set in blood!

THE *NEW YORK TIMES*, NOVEMBER 3, 1859

John Brown's Speech

If any doubts still linger in the minds of thoughtful men as to the real character and aims of John Brown, or as to the best way of dealing with his crime, they must surely be resolved on the reading of his brief speech, made before sentence was passed upon him by the Court. . . .

Brown's speech classifies him at once, and in a class of one. He is a fanatic; *sui generis*. He shows neither the sophistical grasp of mind nor the malignant unfairness of temper which would be necessary to rank him with agitators of theoretical Abolitionism like Wendell Phillips; not the astute coquetry with explosive passions which alone could affiliate him with Republican Party leaders. He is simply John Brown, of Kansas; a man logical after the narrow fashion of the Puritan individualism; a law unto himself, and a believer with all his might in theological abstractions as applied to human society and politics. He hates Slavery, and thinks all slaves ought to be free. That anybody should think it wrong for him, so hating Slavery and so thinking, to attempt to set free the greatest possible number of slaves in the shortest possible time; or that any organization which may appear to him necessary for carrying out this object should be regarded as treasonable, John Brown cannot understand now that he is to be hung for it, any more than we believe he understood it when he made up his mind to set about the work, and others flocked after him, who now, less brave than he, endeavor to throw their own more rational guilt upon his shoulders. We own ourselves at a loss to see in what way the execution of such a man can be so brought about that it may not be converted to the inflammatory purposes of sectional partisans with whom John Brown has plainly nothing in common; and who will be as eager to make him a profitable martyr when dead, as they are to repudiate him while he still lives.

THE *NEW YORK TIMES*, DECEMBER 3, 1859

The Execution of Brown

John Brown has paid the penalty of his crime. He was executed yesterday according to appointment, with due solemnity and under a very imposing display of the military strength of the State of Virginia. The event created a good deal of feeling throughout the country. Our columns contain notices of meetings and other indications of sympathy, held in various sections of the Northern States. In this City two churches were opened for public service—one the Shiloh Church of colored worshipers, and the other the church of Dr. Cheever. No other public demonstration took place here, and even at these churches the attendance was not large. In other places, according to our advices, a very small minority only of the people took part in these public proclamations of sympathy. In both branches of the Massachusetts Legislature a motion to adjourn received but a very meagre support. Half a dozen individuals, in any village, it must be borne in mind, can hold a meeting, or ring bells, or fire minute guns, and so attract as much attention at a distance as if the whole population had been engaged in the affair.

It is but just to add, however, that hundreds and thousands of persons in this City and throughout the North, were deeply moved by personal sympathy for Brown who were still too thoroughly convinced of the legal justice of his execution, to make any outward show of their commisseration [*sic*]. There is not, as we have had occasion to say repeatedly, any general or even any considerable sympathy with Brown's invasion of Virginia or with the object which took him there, in the North. But there is a very wide and profound conviction in the public mind that he was personally honest and sincere,—that his motives were such as he deemed honorable and righteous, and that he believed himself to be doing a religious duty in the work which he undertook. And the public heart always weighs the motives, as well as the acts, of men,—and gives its compassion and its pity freely to the man who stakes everything upon the performance of what he believes to be his duty. We do not believe that one-tenth of the people of the Northern States would assent to the justice of Brown's views of duty, or deny that he had merited the penalty which has overtaken his offence. But we have just as little doubt that a majority of them pity his fate and respect his memory, as that of a brave, conscientious and misguided man.

Now that the curtain has fallen upon this sad tragedy, we trust the public feeling will resume a healthier tone, especially in the Southern States, where it has risen to an unreasonable and a perilous heat. . . .

So far as this outbreak of violent sentiment has been the work of partisans, it is quite useless to protest against it. Some of these men aim at disunion, and they naturally avail themselves of every opportunity to stimulate the distrust, resentment and hatred of the two sections towards each other. Others among them aim only at the ascendancy of their own sectional party in the national councils; and they use these incidents merely to unite the South and coerce the North into conformity to their desires. And still another class aim merely to crush some local competitor, or overbear some local clique, by arousing a public sentiment powerful enough to sweep away all who hesitate about yielding to its current. As these men are thoroughly and recklessly selfish in their aims, no considerations of the public good would check their insane endeavors. It is their determination to goad the South into the conviction that the whole North is bent on waging active war upon Slavery in the Southern States, and that John Brown's troop was only the advanced guard of the general army. They deliberately and willfully falsify the sentiment of the North upon this subject. They represent the Northern people as all Abolitionists,—all fanatics,—all reckless of Southern rights and Southern interests,—all ready to plunge Southern society into the horrors of anarchy and servile insurrection. Whatever ministers to this belief is lavishly used for that purpose; whatever corrects it, is ignored or discredited. The harangues of Phillips, the sermons of Cheever, the diatribes of our Abolition orators and journalists, are greedily copied in Southern prints and put forward as illustrations of Northern sentiment; while the conservative declarations which emanate from our pulpits, our rostrums, and our presses, are utterly unnoticed. We cannot wonder that, under such tuition and discipline, the people of the South, come to regard every Northern man as their enemy. . . .

14

A Divisive Issue: Partisan Responses

On December 14, less than two weeks after Brown was hung, the Senate appointed a bipartisan investigating committee to ascertain the facts relating to the invasion and to determine whether any citizen of the United States was "implicated in, or accessory thereto, by contributions of arms, money, ammunition or otherwise." The Senate debate surrounding the creation of the committee offers a good index of the reactions of political leaders to Brown and his raid. The responses divided along party lines; the Democrats attempted to implicate Republicans in the raid and Republicans sought to disassociate themselves from Brown's act without reneging on their commitment to fight slavery legally. Out on the speaker's circuit, Abraham Lincoln faced the same dilemma.

The Senate committee heard testimony from thirty-two witnesses—including the evasive Howe and Stearns—and issued its report in June, 1860. The majority report, authored by Chairman James M. Mason, found no direct evidence of conspiracy but implied that the raid was the logical outcome of Republican doctrines. Unwilling to let this conclusion stand unchallenged, the two committee Republicans issued a minority report which stated, in part: "We insist, however, that there is no such matter presented in the testimony or existing in fact, as is more than intimated in the report, that even the abolitionists in the free States take courses intended, covertly, to produce forcible violations of the laws and peace of the slave-holding States, much less that any such course is countenanced by the body of the people in the free states."

REMARKS OF SENATOR HENRY WILSON TO THE U.S. SENATE, DECEMBER 6, 1859 [1]

Now, sir, the Senator from Virginia [Mr. Hunter] has alluded to the public sentiment of the country. I believe I utter but the sentiment of all Senators around me from the free States when I say, that when the intelligence of this movement was first received, it was regarded by the public press and by the people as a strike of the workmen at the armory. When the intelligence came of its real character, it was received by the press and the people with emotions of sincere and profound regret. But, sir, an election was pending in the States of New Jersey and New York, and, for mere partisan purposes, one or two papers in the city of New York opened the most violent assault and made the most false and infamous charges against public men and the masses of the people in the free States. This course excited universal indignation. That such charges were made against men who never dreamed of a thing of that kind, excited and aroused the people. I venture to say that not one in ten thousand of the people of the free States ever dreamed that such a movement was on foot or knew anything about it or had any connection with it, and they felt outraged by the cruel and unjust accusations made against the people of the free States.

It was my fortune to spend two or three weeks in the States of New York and New Jersey pending that election. I never saw a man in either of these States, during that canvass, who did not regret it. The leader of that movement at Harper's Ferry, by his bearing, his courage, his words, his acts, has excited the deepest sympathy of many men, and extorted the admiration of all, during his trial and during all the scenes that have since taken place. I believe that to be the sentiment of the country generally. Men believed that he was sincere, that he had violated the law, but that he had followed out his deepest and sincerest convictions, and was willing to take the consequences of his acts. Then, to add to all the rest, the present Govenor of Virginia, by his mode of dealing with this question, by his evident attempt to make political capital out of it, by his effort to get up a panic and to make a parade, has excited a feeling of derision and contempt among the masses of the people. In my judgement, the sympathy and the popular feeling

[1] From *The Congressional Globe* (Washington, D.C., 1860), p. 11. Senator Wilson was a Republican from Massachusetts.

manifested towards John Brown are owing more to the conduct of Governor Wise than to any other source whatever. . . .

REMARKS OF SENATOR JEFFERSON DAVIS TO THE U.S. SENATE, DECEMBER 8, 1859 [2]

. . . I will show before I am done that Seward, by his own declaration, knew of the Harper's Ferry affair. If I succeed in showing that, then he, like John Brown, deserves, I think, the gallows, for his participation in it. (Applause.)

Says Mr. Seward: "There is a meaning in all these facts, which it becomes us to study well. The nation has advanced another stage; it has reached the point where intervention by the Government, for slavery and slave States, will no longer be tolerated."

What is that stage to which the Union has advanced? The slave States had a majority in both branches of Congress once, whereas now the free States are seventeen, and the slave States only fifteen in this Union. There has been a transfer of the majorities in Congress from the slave to the free States. The Government, Senator Seward tells us, has advanced another stage. The Government is no longer to intervene in favor of protection for our slaves. We may be robbed of our property, and the General Government will not intervene for our protection. When the Government gets into the hands of the Republican party, the arm of the General Government, we are told, will not be raised for the protection of our slave property. Then intervention in favor of slavery and slave States will no longer be tolerated. We may be invaded, and the Black Republican Government will stand and permit our soil to be violated and our people assailed and raise no arm in our defense. The sovereignty of the State is no longer to be a bar to encroachments upon our rights when the Government gets into Black Republican hands. Then John Brown, and a thousand John Browns, can invade us, and the Government will not protect us. There will be no army, no navy, sent out to resist such an invasion; but we will be left to the tender mercies of our enemies. Has the South then no right to complain? Has the South then no right to entertain apprehensions when we are told that we are not to be protected in our property when the Republican party shall get possession of the Government? You even declare you will not defend the sovereignty of the States. Have we then no right to announce upon this floor

[2] Ibid., p. 69. Davis was a Democrat from Mississippi.

that if we are not to be protected in our property and sovereignty, we are therefore released from our allegiance, and will protect ourselves out of the Union, if we cannot protect them in the Union? Have we no right to allege that to secure our rights and protect our honor we will dissever the ties that bind us together, even if it rushes us into a sea of blood. . . .

Again, that Senator said: "Free labor has at last apprehended its rights, its interests, its powers, and its destiny and is organizing itself to assume the Government of the Republic. It will henceforth meet you boldly and resolutely here,"—That is on the floor of the Senate—"in the Territories or out of them, wherever you may go to extend slavery. It has driven you back in California and Kansas; it will invade you soon in Delaware, Maryland, Virginia, Missouri, and Texas."

Ah! "it will invade you soon in Delaware and Virginia." Has it not already been done? Has it not invaded us with pike, with spear, with rifles—yes, with Sharpe's rifles? Have not your murderers already come within the limits of our borders, as announced by the traitor, Seward, that it would be done in a short time. At the time of the speech Forbes was in Washington, and he says he communicated to Seward the fact that an invasion would be made. We have been invaded; and that invasion, and the facts connected with it, show Mr. Seward to be a traitor, and deserving of the gallows. (Applause in the galleries.) Brown had organized his constitution when that speech was made; Forbes was in the city of Washington then, and had a conversation with Seward in reference to the invasion. Seward denies that Forbes told him anything about it; but he admits that he had a conversation with Forbes, and that Forbes wanted money. Well, what was that money wanted for? The Senator confesses he had a conversation with Brown about that time. Forbes says it was about the Virginia invasion, and Seward announces in the Senate that Maryland and Virginia would be invaded.

Are these facts not startling? And ought they not to awaken an apprehension in the minds of southern men? Is it not time that we were armed? But, more than that, gentlemen, he goes on to say: "That invasion will be not merely harmless, but beneficent, if you yield seasonably to its just and moderated demands."

That is exactly what John Brown said. He said if we would allow him to take our niggers off without making any fuss about it, he would not kill anybody. (Laughter.) Brown said he did not mean to kill anybody; Seward says it is harmless and beneficent to us if we yield to their just demands. But if we do not yield, what then? Why, Brown said he would kill our people, butcher our women and children. What does Seward say? "Whether that consummation shall be allowed to take effect and with needful and wise precautions against sudden change and disaster, or be hurried on by violence, is all that remains for you (the people of the South) to decide."

That is the very language of John Brown. Whether we will allow them to do it quietly or not, is the only question for the South to decide. Virginia has decided it, and has hung the traitor Brown; and may, if she can get a chance, hang the traitor Seward. (Laughter.) We have repeatedly refused to yield, and you have sought to force us to yield by violence, and Virginia has met it with violence, and has hung the man; and Virginia has had twenty-five hundred men under arms, and has defied all your efforts to rescue him.

REMARKS OF STEPHEN DOUGLAS TO THE U.S. SENATE, JANUARY 23, 1860 [3]

. . . It cannot be said with truth that the Harper's Ferry case will not be repeated, or is not in danger of repetition. It is only necessary to inquire into the causes which produced the Harper's Ferry outrage, and ascertain whether those causes are yet in active operation, and then you can determine whether there is any ground for apprehension that that invasion will be repeated. Sir, what were the causes which produced the Harper's Ferry outrage? Without stopping to adduce evidence in detail, I have no hesitation in expressing my firm and deliberate conviction that the Harper's Ferry crime was the natural, logical, inevitable result of the doctrines and teachings of the Republican party, as explained and enforced in their platform, their partisan presses, their pamphlets and books, and especially in the speeches of their leaders in and out of Congress. (Applause in the galleries.) . . .

. . . I am not making this statement for the purpose of crimination or partisan effect. I desire to call the attention of the members of that party to a reconsideration of the doctrines that they are in the habit of enforcing, with a view to a fair judgement whether they do not lead directly to those consequences on the part of those deluded persons who think that all they say is meant in real earnest and ought to be carried out. The great principle that underlies the

[3] Ibid., pp. 553–54. Douglas was a Democrat from Illinois.

organization of the Republican party is violent, irreconcilable, eternal warfare upon the institution of American slavery, with the view of its ultimate extinction throughout the land; sectional war is to be waged until the cotton fields of the South shall be cultivated by free labor, or the rye fields of New York and Massachusetts shall be cultivated by slave labor. In furtherance of this article of their creed, you find their political organization not only sectional in its location, but one whose vitality consists in appeals to northern passion, northern prejudice, northern ambition against southern States, southern institutions, and southern people. . . .

Can any man say to us that although this outrage has been perpetrated at Harper's Ferry, there is no danger of its recurrence? Sir, is not the Republican party still embodied, organized, confident of success and defiant in its pretensions? Does it not now hold and proclaim the same creed that it did before this invasion? It is true that most of its representatives here disavow the acts of John Brown at Harper's Ferry. I am glad that they do so; I am rejoiced that they have gone thus far; but I must be permitted to say to them that it is not sufficient that they disavow the act, unless they also repudiate and denounce the doctrines and teachings which produced the act. Those doctrines remain the same; those teachings are being poured into the minds of men throughout the country by means of speeches and pamphlets and books and through partisan presses. The causes that produced the Harper's Ferry invasion are now in active operation. . . .

ABRAHAM LINCOLN, COOPER UNION ADDRESS, FEBRUARY 27, 1860 [4]

You charge that we stir up insurrections among your slaves. We deny it; and what is your proof? Harper's Ferry! John Brown!! John Brown was no Republican; and you have failed to implicate a single Republican in his Harper's Ferry enterprise. If any member of our party is guilty in that matter, you know it or you do not know it. If you do know it, you are inexcusable for not designating the man and proving the fact. If you do not know it, you are inexcusable for asserting it, and especially for persisting in the assertion after you have tried and failed to make the proof. You need

---

[4] From "The Address of the Hon. Abraham Lincoln . . . Delivered at Cooper Institute" (New York: George F. Nesbitt & Co., 1860), pp. 21–23, 24–25.

not be told that persisting in a charge which one does not know to be true, is simply malicious slander.

Some of you admit that no Republican designedly aided or encouraged the Harper's Ferry affair; but still insist that our doctrines and declarations necessarily lead to such results. We do not believe it. We know we hold to no doctrine, and make no declaration, which were not held to and made by "our fathers who framed the Government under which we live." You never dealt fairly by us in relation to this affair. When it occurred, some important State elections were near at hand, and you were in evident glee with the belief that, by charging the blame upon us, you could get an advantage of us in those elections. The elections came, and your expectations were not quite fulfilled. Every Republican man knew that, as to himself at least, your charge was a slander, and he was not much inclined by it to cast his vote in your favor. Republican doctrines and declarations are accompanied with a continual protest against any interference whatever with your slaves, or with you about your slaves. Surely, this does not encourage them to revolt. True, we do, in common with "our fathers, who framed the Government under which we live," declare our belief that slavery is wrong; but the slaves do not hear us declare even this. For anything we say or do, the slaves would scarcely know there is a Republican party. I believe they would not, in fact, generally know it but for your misrepresentations of us, in their hearing. In your political contests among yourselves, each faction charges the other with sympathy with Black Republicanism; and then, to give point to the charge, defines Black Republicanism to simply be insurrection, blood and thunder among the slaves. . . .

John Brown's effort was peculiar. It was not a slave insurrection. It was an attempt by white men to get up a revolt among slaves, in which the slaves refused to participate. In fact, it was so absurd that the slaves, with all their ignorance, saw plainly enough it could not succeed. That affair, in its philosophy, corresponds with the many attempts, related in history, at the assassination of kings and emperors. An enthusiast broods over the oppression of a people till he fancies himself commissioned by Heaven to liberate them. He ventures the attempt, which ends in little else than his own execution. Orsini's attempt on Louis Napoleon, and John Brown's attempt at Harper's Ferry were, in their philosophy, precisely the same. The eagerness to cast blame on old England in the one case, and on New England in the other, does not disprove the sameness of the two things.

And how much would it avail you, if you could, by the use of John Brown, Helper's Book, and the like, break up the Republican organization? Human action can be modified to some extent, but human nature cannot be changed. There is a judgment and a feeling against slavery in this nation, which cast at least a million and a half of votes. You cannot destroy that judgment and feeling —that sentiment—by breaking up the political organization which rallies around it. You can scarcely scatter and disperse an army which has been formed into order in the face of your heaviest fire; but if you could, how much would you gain by forcing the sentiment which created it out of the peaceful channel of the ballot-box into some other channel? What would that other channel probably be? Would the number of John Browns be lessened or enlarged by the operation?

PART THREE

JOHN BROWN IN HISTORY

The last seven selections represent a range of often conflicting historical interpretations of Brown and his raid. Working from different perspectives and preconceptions and with different concerns, the historians, like Brown's contemporaries, assess his personality, motives, plan, immediate impact, and legacy in a variety of ways.

15

James Schouler (1891)

Most nineteenth-century commentaries on Brown were biographies or memoirs written by men like Sanborn, Redpath, Stearns, and Douglass, who knew the man and wrote glowingly of his life and work in which they had participated or observed first-hand. James Schouler, who received his A.B. from Harvard in the year that John Brown raided Harper's Ferry, was one of the first to take a detached look at Brown, in the context of a comprehensive history. A prominent lawyer as well as historian, Schouler wrote five volumes on the United States from the Revolution to the Civil War; two later volumes, published in 1899 and 1913, carried the narrative through the war and reconstruction. In his treatment of Brown, Schouler combines a skeptical attitude toward the man and the raid with an abiding appreciation for the lessons of his self-sacrifice.[1]

It was just after the October elections that a cry of horror was heard through the land. Virginia, the mother of States, was in-

[1] From James Schouler, *History of the United States of America Under the Constitution* (New York, 1891) 5: 437–39, 440–41, 443–44. Footnotes have been been omitted.

vaded by a Northern horde; the national arsenal seized at Harper's
Ferry; slavery assaulted on soil which the Federal Constitution held
sacred; and a servile war inaugurated, that blacks might ravish,
despoil, and murder. In the agitated condition of the Southern
mind the danger was easily exaggerated; and at the first alarm it
seemed as if the whole abolition army above the border, and med-
dlesome civilization itself, were in active motion to start the "irrepressible conflict." This panic subsided when the self-imprisoned
invaders were secured with chains or shot dead, and the lanterns
of investigation, prying from top to bottom and from corner to
corner, revealed nothing more serious than a foolish and crack-
brained plot; and the invading cohorts of "Black Republican" cut-
throats and incendiaries dwindled down to a little band of twenty-
two men, armed with rifles, pistols, and pikes,—a family party for
the most part, with a few companions, white and black,—all headed
by that obscure patriarch and self-appointed scourge of the Almighty, old John Brown.

Had this sporadic and nonsensical movement been calmly and
considerately viewed by those against whom it was directed, had the
pitiful and deluded assailants been treated with the decent magnanimity for which so good an opportunity was afforded, John Brown's
raid would have passed out of the public mind, like any other
nine-days' wonder, and been forgotten. No negro uprising followed,
nor the shadow of a servile war; the negro continued as docile, the
Constitution as stringent in its protection of slave property as
slavery could ever have expected. But the slave master showed on
this occasion his innate tyranny and cruelty towards an adversary,
by something of that gloating vengeance which our English code
once inflicted when it quartered and disembowelled political traitors; and had the ill-calculating liberator dared the laws in one of
the lower cotton States, instead of mild Virginia, there is little
doubt that he would have been much more ignominiously dealt
with. John Brown was arrested, tried, and convicted in hot haste;
he was strung up on the gallows-tree; and meeting death like a
gallant man who believes his cause to be right, he became a martyr,
and consequently an inspiration and a figure in history.

Of Pilgrim pedigree and revolutionary fighting stock, our grim
hero was one of those stern-faced sons of righteousness who read
their Bible, rear great families of sons and daughters, and fight
poverty's privations handicapped, with every chance of worldly
success against them. John Brown's very name, rugged and familiar

on the tongue, claims kin for him with a host of common people of English blood. Failing in one means of livelihood after another, he settled with his family on a farm among the lonely Adirondacks, where, under the countenance of that rich philanthropist, Gerrit Smith, he managed a scheme for the amelioration of free blacks, which, like most others to which he laid his unlucky hand, turned out badly. Kansas and the struggle to found a free State sent four of his children westward among the first settlers. The father followed with other sons in 1856, not as a peaceable farmer, but to put cold lead into the border ruffians. Brown's inflexible temper and fierceness by this time made him an unsafe man for those pioneer surroundings; his range of vision was necessarily narrow; and, already an honest hater of slavery, whose only patrons were avowed abolitionists, he was almost crazed in mind by the sufferings which his sons were forced to undergo while the prairie turbulence was at its height. The old man was a thorn to Robinson and the other leaders of the free-State party, whose methods were politic, and who aimed to carry their point. He swung "the sword of the Lord and Gideon;" he conceived bloody plans with cunning reticence, and executed them with stolid disregard of the general opinion. His night massacre near Pottawatomie, where with his little band he pulled unoffending people out of their beds and put them to death because they were slaveholders, was the one atrocity of 1856 on freedom's side which could never be expiated. . . .

. . . Though of decided character, his mind had been strangely unstrung by the murderous scenes in Kansas in which he had borne a part. . . . We must think his faculties so strained and distorted as to lose all just sense of the adequacy of means to his ends. Insanity ran in Brown's family, and one of his sons in Kansas was a victim of the malady. Yet monomaniacs may plot most cunningly; their folly develops more properly at the stage of action. What moonlight madness do we see in that constitution drawn up and read to confederates over the Canadian border, wherein John Brown announces the provisional government of the United States which he intends, as the new Cromwell, to establish. And what quintessence of nonsense is curtained in that night descent of scarcely twenty confederates upon Harper's Ferry from the neighboring heights of Maryland, where the Browns, father and sons, under the equally plebeian name of Smith, had rented their small farm the past summer, and stealthily collected weapons of war enough to deck out half a regiment, and hard cash amounting to two hundred and fifty dollars. Any town of five thousand inhabitants ought, one would think, to have disarmed this amateur array; and any United States arsenal, in which were usually stored a hundred thousand stand of arms, should not, except in slack Virginia, have been left so utterly unguarded. John Brown makes the public property his own without firing a gun, and with sublimated zeal posts guards on the railway bridge near by, and makes a night arrest of two slave-owning farmers. So far does the Cromwell strategy sustain him; but when he stops the midnight train, and then suffers it, with chivalrous expressions, to go on its way towards Baltimore, why does he not scud like the fox to the near mountain covert, instead of returning complacently with his pike-bearers into the premises of which he has robbed thirty millions of people, and barring the outer doors? With the nation's capital not so many miles away, and steam and telegraph spreading the alarm through the small hours of the night, it is not strange that morning overwhelms the whole crazy exploit. . . .

John Brown was no Cæsar, no Cromwell, but a plain citizen of a free republic, whom distressing events drove into a fanaticism to execute purposes to which he was incompetent. He detested slavery, and that detestation led him to take up arms not only against slavery, but against that public opinion which was slowly formulating how best to eradicate it. Woe to the conquered. The North made no appeals for that clemency which slaveholders had alone to consider. Brown had not been lenient to masters, nor were masters bound to be lenient to him. And yet Brown was an enthusiast, and not a felon; the essence of his crime was unselfish. Like the French country maiden who went to Paris to plunge her dagger into a bloody ruler's heart, he meant to rescue good morals from the usurpation of human laws. Corday fulfilled her solitary plan because it was reasonable; John Brown failed in his plan because it was unreasonable; but both, as actors and martyrs, flashing upon the world's attention like new meteors, left examples of self-sacrifice, the one upon the guillotine, and the other upon the gallows, which a people could not refrain from exalting. The virgin damsel of grace and beauty, and the grim old man of sixty, stern and sanguinary, who led on his sons, take equal hold of posterity's imagination; of each one it has been said, by acute observers, that the immediate effect of their deeds was injurious to politics; and yet society in the long centuries is stronger for being thus taught that despotism over fellow-men is not safely hedged in by authority.

Brown's stalwart, unique, and spectral figure led on, grotesque but terribly in earnest, the next time Virginia's soil was invaded,—not, however, for executing any such unfeasible scheme of making the slaves their own avengers, but to apply the war powers of the nation against disloyal masters.

16

Oswald Garrison Villard (1910)

Oswald Garrison Villard, a grandson of William Lloyd Garrison, wrote the first scholarly account of Brown's life a half-century after the Harper's Ferry raid. This well-researched volume was undertaken by the author in an attempt to present a balanced account of Brown, "free from bias, from the errors in taste and fact of the mere panegyrist, and from the blind prejudice of those who can see in John Brown nothing but a criminal." Villard's book brings out new details about Brown and the raid and is, on the whole, a positive treatment of its subject. Villard's sympathy colors his assessment as he allows the favorable self-portrayal of Brown's prison letters to outweigh the sordid events in Brown's earlier career.[1]

Now, fifty years later, it is possible to take an unbiased view of John Brown and his achievements, even if opinions as to his true character and moral worth diverge almost as violently as in 1859. There are those in the twentieth century, appointed to teach history in high places, who are so blind as to see in John Brown only the murderer of the Pottawatomie, a "horse-thief and midnight assassin." Still others behold in him not merely a sainted martyr of the most elevated character, but the liberator of Kansas, and the man who, unaided, struck their chains from the limbs of more than three million human beings. These writers would leave nothing to be credited to Abraham Lincoln, nothing to the devoted band of uncompromising Abolitionists who, for thirty years prior to Harper's Ferry, had gone up and down the North denouncing slavery in its every form, stirring the public conscience and preparing the popular mind for what was to come. The truth lies between these two extremes. Were men who have powerfully moulded their time to be judged solely by their errors, however

[1] From Oswald Garrison Villard, *John Brown, 1800–59: A Biography Fifty Years After* (Boston: Houghton, Mifflin, and Company, 1910), pp. 586–89.

grievous, all history would wear a different aspect. In Virginia, John Brown atoned for Pottawatomie by the nobility of his philosophy and his sublime devotion to principle, even to the gallows. As inexorable a fate as ever dominated a Greek tragedy guided this life. He walked always as one blindfolded. Something compelled him to attack slavery by force of arms, and to that impulse he yielded, reckoning not at all as to the outcome, and making not the slightest effort to plan beyond the first blow. Without foresight, strategy or generalship, he entered the Harper's Ferry trap confident that all was for the best, to be marvellously preserved from the sabre which, had it gone home, must have rendered barren his entire life, his sacrifice and his devotion.

When Brown assailed slavery in Virginia, the outlook for Abolition was never so hopeful. The "irrepressible conflict" was never so irrepressible, and he who believes there would have been no forcible abolition of slavery had there been no John Brown, is singularly short-sighted. The South was on the brink of a volcano the day before the blow at Harper's Ferry, as it was the day after, because slavery was intolerable morally and economically. It was bound to be overthrown because, in the long run, truth and righteousness prevail. Helper's book was written before John Brown struck, and the facts it contained, as to the social and economic injury to the South from its system of unpaid labor, lost and gained nothing by the bloodshed at the Harper's Ferry arsenal or the deaths on the Charlestown scaffold. The secession movement was too far under way for any peaceable solution; the minds of too many Southern leaders besides Governor Wise were thoroughly committed to it even before the raid. "The truth is," wrote Alexander Stephens on November 30, 1860, "our leaders and public men . . . do not desire to continue it [the Union] on any terms. They do not wish any redress of wrongs, they are disunionists *per se* and avail themselves of present circumstances to press their object." This feeling and that sense of personal hostility which, as Senator Iverson remarked in the following month, kept the Northern Senators on their side of the Senate "sullen and gloomy" while "we sit on our side with portentous scowls. . . . We are enemies as much as if we were hostile States,"—all this was not the outgrowth of a year's excitement, nor did it begin in the John Brown raid. There was seething bitterness when the Kansas-Nebraska act was passed. There were two hostile camps when Sumner was struck down and one side of the Senate mourned, while the other exulted.

In 1859, the public recognized in John Brown a fanatic, but one of those fanatics who, by their readiness to sacrifice their lives, are forever advancing the world. Plenty exclaimed, like George Hoadley: "Poor old John Brown, God sanctify his death to our good, and give us a little of his courage, piety and self-sacrificing spirit, with more brains!" They saw that he had no personal ambition; they felt that he was brave, kind, honest, truth-telling and God-revering. The nature of the conflict before the country was thereby revealed to them, and the revelation advanced the conflict immeasurably, just as it stirred the slave-power to new aggressions. It was like the lightning from the sky that lights up the darkness of the coming storm, so that men may for a fraction of a second take measure of its progress. So even across the water it illuminated the heavens to Victor Hugo and let him look so far into the future that he wrote:

> The gaze of Europe is fixed at this moment on America. . . . The hangman of Brown—let us speak plainly—the hangman of Brown will be neither District-Attorney Hunter, nor Judge Parker, nor Governor Wise, nor the little State of Virginia, but—you shudder to think it and to give it utterance—the whole great American Republic. . . . It will open a latent fissure that will finally split the Union asunder. The punishment of John Brown may consolidate slavery in Virginia, but it will certainly shatter the American Democracy. You preserve your shame but you kill your glory.

It was to Victor Hugo, too, the "assassination of Deliverance by Liberty."

But the true Deliverance came with John Brown behind the bars at Charlestown, when there was suddenly revealed to him how inferior a weapon was the sword he had leaned upon from the time he had abandoned the pursuits of peace for has warfare on slavery. Not often in history is there recorded such a rise to spiritual greatness of one whose hands were so stained with blood, whose judgment was ever so faulty, whose public career was so brief. John Brown is and must remain a great and lasting figure in American history. Not, however, because he strove to undo one wrong by committing another; not because he took human lives in a vain effort to end the sacrifice of other lives and souls entailed by slavery. Judged by the ordinary legal and moral standards, John Brown's life was forfeit after Harper's Ferry. The methods by which he essayed to achieve reforms are never to be justified until two wrongs make a right. It was the weapon of the spirit by which he finally conquered. In its power lies not only the secret of his influence, and his immortality, but the finest ethical teachings of a life which, for all its faults, inculcates many an enduring lesson, and will forever make its appeal to the imagination. His brief, yet everlasting, prison life is the clearest condemnation of his violent methods both in Kansas and in Virginia. For the Abolitionists, it will be remembered, he had had nothing but contempt. Theirs were "but words, words"; yet it was by words, and words, embodying his moral principles, the theological teachings he valued so highly, the doctrines of the Saviour, who knew no distinction of race, creed or color, and by the beauty of his own peace of spirit in the face of death, that he stirred his Northern countrymen to their depths and won the respect even of the citizens of the South. It was in jail that he discovered, too, how those very words of the Abolition preachers he had despised had prepared and watered the soil so that his own seed now fell upon fertile fields, took root, and sprouted like the magic plants of children's fables.

Thus it came about that when the men of the North, within an amazingly brief space of time, found themselves, to their astonishment, likewise compelled to go South with arms in their hands, it was not the story of bloody Pottawatomie, nor of the battle at Osawatomie, that thrilled them, nor even of the dauntless lion at bay in the engine house. It was the man on the scaffold sacrificing, not taking life, who inspired. The song that regiment after regiment sang at Charlestown dealt not with John Brown's feeble sword, but with his soul. It was the heroic qualities of his spirit that awed them, his wonderful readiness to die with joy and in peace, as so many of them were about to die for the nation and the freedom of another race. They, too, were giving up all that was dear to them, their wives, their children, the prospect of happy homes and long, useful lives, to march and suffer; to see their brothers, yea their sons, fall by their side; even to receive upon their own bodies the sabres of their enemies. Theirs, too, was the enobling experience of self-sacrifice. How great, then, must have been their inspiration, to feel that he who was the first in America to die for a treason which became as if overnight the highest form of devotion to an inspired cause, was marching on in the realms above!

And so, wherever there is battling against injustice and oppression, the Charlestown gallows that became a cross will help men to live and die. The story of John Brown will ever confront the spirit of despotism, when men are struggling to throw off the shackles of social or political or physical slavery. His own country, while admitting his mistakes without undue palliation or excuse, will forever acknowledge the divine that was in him by the side of what was human and faulty, and blind and wrong. It will cherish the memory of the prisoner of Charlestown in 1859 as at once a sacred, a solemn and an inspiring American heritage.

17

Hill Peebles Wilson (1913)

*Two of the historical works most critical of John
Brown have come out of Kansas: Hill Peebles Wilson's* John
Brown, Soldier of Fortune: A Critique, *and James C.* Malin's
John Brown and the Legend of Fifty-Six. *Whereas Malin, concentrating on the Kansas years, viewed Brown as a frontier
thief and inveterate liar whose role in Kansas affairs had been
elevated out of all proportion to his actual significance, Wilson portrayed him essentially as a villain, motivated at every
stage of his life by avarice. In arguing this thesis with respect
to Harper's Ferry, Wilson identified Brown and Hugh Forbes
as two of a kind—thereby linking Brown to a man whom
even pro-Brown biographers acknowledged to be an adventurer seeking personal gain.*

*Wilson devoted much of his book to a critique of works
sympathetic to Brown, particularly the biography by Villard,
whose alleged distortions Wilson set out to correct. In offering
a new assessment of Brown, however, Wilson in fact produced
a virulent polemic against him. But despite its obvious bias,
this book does address a central issue: which is the real John
Brown—the "outlaw" of Kansas or the "martyr" of Harper's
Ferry?* [1]

The picturesque figure which has been presented to the public
as John Brown is an historical myth—a fiction. The character, as
it has been exploited, is a contradiction of the laws that govern in
human nature. The material for it was furnished by partisans,
who were unscrupulous writers of the times of strenuous political
excitement and national unrest, in which Brown, by his deeds of
violence, attracted public attention. Following the practice of partisans, these writers wrote with reckless disregard for the truth of
their statements. Later, in the ultimate crisis that occurred in his

[1] From Hill Peebles Wilson, *John Brown, Soldier of Fortune: A Critique*
(Lawrence, Kansas: Hill P. Wilson, 1913), pp. 26–27, 400–402, 405–407. Footnotes
have been omitted.

fortunes, he was eulogized in surpassing eloquence by sincere people
of high ideals, who were unaware of the real character of the object of their adoration. They were not informed concerning the
criminal life which he had led, or of the shockingly brutal crimes
which he had committed; neither did they understand that in his
final undertaking he sought to involve a section of our fair land in
a carnival of rapine and bloodshed exceeding in extent the horrors
of San Domingo. They were misled and were moved, in their
orations, solely by sentiment and misplaced sympathy. Instead of a
grim and unscrupulous soldier of fortune, leading a band of
desperate men in an effort to unloose in the Slave States the demon
of insurrection, they could see in him only a religious devotee,
whom their imaginations had created; whose life they believed had
been a devotion to deeds of charity and benevolence; who for years
had been the especial champion of the slave; and whose work in
Kansas had been, as in the existing crisis, an heroic and consistent
consecration to duty. . . .

At the head of the schedule of assumptions concerning the innocence of Brown's intentions, the purity of his motives, and the
exaltation of his devotion to humanity, is his "martyrdom." This
item has been illuminated with a halo of holiness. As "Christ died
to make men holy," so Brown is said to have died to "make men
free." No one has claimed that Hugh Forbes was an humanitarian,
or other than an adventurer. Yet in relation to Brown's insurrection, the minds of the two men—John Brown and Hugh Forbes—
met in full accord; there was agreement between them. Together
they planned the invasion of the South, for the promotion of their
personal fortunes. Their aims, their ambitions, and their hopes were
identical. If Brown's exchequer had been ample, Forbes too would
have appeared at Harper's Ferry and there would have been a pair
of martyrs there: "Two of a kind."

The logic of the fiction of his martyrdom is founded upon the
assumption that Brown held an option upon his life which he
elected to forfeit; and that he offered it as a sacrifice: that he chose
to die, as the Redeemer of Men died; and in thus dying made "the
gallows glorious like the cross." Brown did not contemplate dying
at Harper's Ferry any more than did Hugh Forbes, or Stevens, or
Cook, or Kagi; and he would not have died at Charlestown if he
could have controlled the event. These men knew that some of
them would, probably, die, but each passed the subject over lightly,
believing that in some inscrutable way, if fatalities occurred, it

would be some of the others who would fall. Men of their type "die but once." Brown accepted the chances of war as did his followers, and as Forbes sought the opportunity of doing. Men who have similarly risked their lives, times almost without number, are not impressed by such martyrdoms. To his faithful Sanborn, Brown wrote: "I am now rather anxious to live for a few years." He desired to live to organize, and to command the army of the Provisional Government; and to be the head of a new nation: a new "United States." He hoped for longevity, that he might wear the honors and enjoy the fame and the emoluments of his prospective achievement.

The years of Brown's life were a constant, persistent, strenuous struggle to get money. As to the means which should be employed in the getting of it, he was indifferent. In his philosophy, results were paramount; the means to the end were of no consequence. A stranger to honor, he violated every confidence that should be held sacred among men; and in his avarice trampled upon every law, moral and statute, human and Divine. Consistent with the speculative instinct so distinctly characteristic of his life, his greatest or principal object was to get money, and to get it quickly. . . .

Of Brown, it may be truthfully said that within the limits of his resources, he did nothing in a small way, nor did he move with a faint heart. With him, there was neither halting nor trifling in action. He was consistently an adventurer. His theology scorned all creeds. Without capital he was a plunger among speculators. . . . [W]ithin one year from the date of the outburst of his determination to be freed from poverty, he indulged hopes of a successful conquest: hopes of riches and of fame. An habitual cruelty in his domestic life, . . . nerved his hand to execute the ferocious butchery of his neighbors on the Pottawatomie, and steeled his heart to incite the slaves at Harper's Ferry to emulate the example of Southampton. His attempt at revolution was not the result of a previous conviction and consecration to duty and to the cause of humanity, but of a growth—the indulgence and development of an abnormal passion for speculation: the culmination downward of his speculative and criminal instincts. . . . In the horses owned by the Shermans, and by other well-to-do neighbors, he saw, and grasped, the opportunity—a desperate one—to make a "coup to restore his fortunes." Out of that plunge in robbery and murder came the leader of a gang of horse thieves—the chrysalis of the guerrilla captain of Osawatomie.

Driven out of the Territory by the establishment of order, the crafty marauder raided the East as the militant defender of Kansas. In the practice of his impositions there, he met and established confidential relations with men who plotted against the life of the nation; men who planned how to provoke a revolution; how best to "split the Union"; men who wished "success to every slave insurrection." From this atmosphere, pregnant with the sentiment of disloyalty to the Union, Brown derived the inspiration which encouraged him to plan to do what his mentors had not the courage to undertake. Out of his negotiations with them came money; munitions of war; Hugh Forbes, the revolutionist; mutual planning for a revolution, and a dream of empire.

John Brown will live in history; but his name will not be found among the names of those who have wrought for humanity and for righteousness; or among the names of the martyrs and the saints who "washed their robes and made them white in the blood of the Lamb."

"YET SHALL HE LIVE": but it will be as a soldier of fortune, an adventurer. He will take his place in history as such; and will rank among adventurers as Napoleon ranks among marshals; as Captain Kidd among pirates; and as Jonathan Wild among thieves.

18
Allan Nevins (1950)

The excerpt below is drawn from a comprehensive two-volume study of pre–Civil War America. Allan Nevins is typical of a group of historians writing after World War II who strove for broad narrative coverage and balanced interpretation. Professing no particular ideological preconceptions, Nevins offers perhaps the most objective assessment of Brown's place in the context of his times, and presents an interesting treatment of Brown's "reasoning insanity." [1]

The fierce-eyed, iron-jawed chieftain, adjuring everyone to constant caution and vigilance, awaited the best hour to strike. When he arrived, he had almost completely matured his plan. It was not what many writers have stated. He did *not* intend to make a sudden raid and then retreat to some mountain bastion. He meant by a sudden blow to take Harper's Ferry, thus (as his daughter put it) striking terror to the slaveholders about; to send agents among the surrounding plantations, rallying the slaves; to hold the town for at least a short time, expecting as many helpers, white and black, from the district as assailants; to prepare for rapid movement *southward;* and, as he moved, to continue sending out armed bands to free more slaves, secure provisions and hostages, and destroy slaveholding morale. He would follow the Appalachians into Tennessee and even Alabama, the heart of the South, making forays into the plains on either side. He had told Forbes that on the first night of the stroke he thought he might get from two to five hundred Negro adherents. As for the militia and regular army, he contemptuously judged them by the specimens he had seen in Kansas. His daughter writes that he deemed them "an inefficient lot." A crazy plan? At any rate, he believed in it intensely. An Ohio friend had expostulated with him in 1858:

[1] From Allan Nevins, *The Emergence of Lincoln* (New York: Charles Scribner's Sons, 1950), II, 73–77. Footnotes have been omitted.

He replied that with a hundred men he could free Kansas and Missouri too, and could march them to Washington and turn the President and Cabinet out of doors. . . . He seemed unable to think of anything else or talk of anything else. This affiant attempted to quiet him and get him into conversation upon other matters, but without success. The Kansas difficulties, the death of his son, and slavery were the only things of which he could be induced to speak. His whole manner and conversation was that of a monomaniac, and upon matters in regard to which he held the conversation, this affiant regarded him as altogether insane; such was his opinion at the time.

News of his proposed attempt to deal a bloody stroke at some Southern community and set a slave revolt ablaze was being awaited with varying degrees of knowledge by his abolitionist backers: Gerrit Smith, George L. Stearns, Theodore Parker, Frank B. Sanborn, Thomas Wentworth Higginson, S. G. Howe, Frederick Douglass, and others. Visiting New England in May, Brown had held frequent meetings with the secret conspiratorial committee; had spoken again in Concord Town House, where he impressed Bronson Alcott and Rockwood Hoar as well as Emerson; and had received a little more than $4,000, of which Sanborn says that at least $3,800 was given with a clear understanding of its future use. Indeed, he intimated frankly to all his intention of levying a blow for freedom, running off as many slaves as he could, and making slavery insecure. Higginson and Douglass knew that he intended to strike at Harper's Ferry.

Servile insurrection, armed strife, wide and continued bloodshed —these were inherent elements of Brown's wild scheme, and he and his fellow-conspirators of the North knew it. In an effort to delude others (and perhaps himself) he had tried to confuse the issue. He had said that his well-controlled blow would *forestall* an inevitable, uncontrollable, and horribly vengeful revolt in the future. He had also told Higginson that he would not foment a slave rebellion at all, but merely get together families and bands of fugitives who would then defend themselves. This was a distinction without a difference. Any widespread attempt by slaves to escape would be insurrection, would be treated by masters and government as such, and would involve fierce combat. What Brown called defensive warfare by slave bands would be called offensive warfare by all Southern whites. According to his follower Realf, Brown spoke of killing no slaveholder, and yet in the same breath talked of fighting off individual opponents, militia, and the Federal army—which meant general killing. It was not for nothing that he had given careful study to the tactics of Toussaint l'Ouverture and Garibaldi. If Gerrit Smith, Sanborn, and the rest did not comprehend that his enterprise would bring on an implacable conflict and a heavy effusion of blood, they were much less acute men than the world esteemed them. The greater Brown's success, the bloodier would be the fighting of whites and blacks, raiders and troops.

The fact was that Higginson and some others actually wanted civil war, and hoped that Brown's raid would precipitate it. For a clergyman, young Higginson had a bloodthirsty mind; for while visiting Kansas in the spring of 1856 he had approved of the killings on the Pottawatomie, and he now avowed himself ready to see slavery extinguished in gore. Brown had told Gerrit Smith, Sanborn, and Higginson how many weapons he had and how he meant to use them. He had written Sanborn: "I expect to effect a mighty conquest, even though it be like the last victory of Samson." Of the conspirators, Parker, Stearns, and Howe knew less about the details of the scheme, and Parker, mortally stricken, had departed for Europe. They were aware, however, that he planned shortly to launch his great scheme of slave-liberation.

For the selection of Harper's Ferry as the point of attack, Brown alone was responsible. He had hesitated as to the place of his stroke, for a time believing that it should be in the Deep South— Anne Brown says that he mentioned Baton Rouge. But he had rejected this idea on grounds of humanity, believing that the "ferocity" of the slaves in the Lower South might prompt them to a wholesale massacre. His notion of the fierce rebelliousness of slaves in the cotton kingdom had been derived from abolitionist publications. Moreover, Harper's Ferry seemed a better point in that he hoped for helpers from Pennsylvania and western Maryland and Virginia. Frederick Douglass had vehemently protested against the choice on strategic grounds, declaring that the town would prove a perfect trap where concentrating forces would swiftly recover the arsenal, cut off the raiders, and kill or capture them. But Brown was immovable.

Members of the attacking party expressed similar fears when Brown first explained the plan to them after they had gathered at the Kennedy farmhouse. Until then, they had believed that he intended merely to repeat on a more ambitious scale the slave-running coup executed in Missouri the previous year. Hearing the leader announce that they were to take the town, garrison the arsenal, armory, and rifle works, and hold them, the men were aghast. A majority, including Brown's three sons, protested that failure was inevitable. The dispute grew heated. "In September it nearly broke up the camp," Charles P. Tidd, a Maine lad who had shared in the Missouri raid, later testified. But the sanguine Cook, busy familiarizing himself with the town, supported the plan; Kagi accepted it, believing they would get out of the pent-up village before troops could be mobilized; and Stevens acquiesced. When Brown told the men that since a majority opposed him he would resign and they could choose another leader, this ultimatum brought them to his side. Several, however, believed they were going to certain death—and one described his own end.

John Brown's whole course showed that, despite statements made by some biographers, he had given up the idea of a swift retreat to some mountain fortress. In the first place, no impregnable eyries, no deep hidden fastnesses, exist anywhere near Harper's Ferry. The district bounded by Winchester, Hagerstown, Frederick, and Fairfax is everywhere passable; it contains no steep cliffs, no chasms, no swamps, no unknown caverns; troops could move through it at will. During the Civil War they did quarter it in every direction, and stormed Maryland Heights opposite the Ferry with ease. Three expert topographical engineers, writing a dozen years later of the mountainous country of Maryland between the Potomac and Pennsylvania, stated that it, "so far from being wild and uninhabitable, contains some of the finest roads and most desirable farms in the State, much of the region being characterized by hills of moderate height whose rounded summits are covered with verdure." The two Virginia and two Maryland counties which environ Harper's Ferry were a rich grain country with a combined population in 1860 of one hundred twelve thousand, three hundred people. No real hiding places were available.

In the second place, Brown never even made a reconnaissance of the surrounding country to familiarize himself with hidden paths and spots of refuge. He knew the road north to Chambersburg, and that was about all. And thirdly, he made no effort in advance to stock or fortify any hill area. To retreat to the Allegheny ridge, some twenty-five miles to the west, without food and water, would have been madness. Any leader contemplating a stand in some recess there would have made a cache of arms and provisions. It is significant that, just before his attack, Brown moved his main stock of weapons—to what point? Not to the hills, but to a schoolhouse about a mile from the Ferry.

Obviously, this military tyro believed that he could hold Harper's Ferry for some time. He expected to be successful in gaining widespread support, and to push forward down the Appalachian chain. If by any chance he was unsuccessful, he might retreat northward into Pennsylvania.

Two factors gave him a certain amount of confidence. He knew upper Maryland and Virginia to be full of people who disliked slavery, the citizens who later held Maryland firm in the Union and who detached West Virginia as a new State; and he believed many would flock to his aid. He was deceived by his Kansas experience into thinking that any border country was a region of sharp antagonism between slaveholding and freesoil elements. At an early date he had taken some steps to inform himself about the antislavery families of Bedford, Chambersburg, Gettysburg, and Carlisle in Pennsylvania, of the Hagerstown district in Maryland, and of the Martinsburg area in Virginia. As the second factor, he believed great numbers of slaves would flock to him. Here he was deceived by abolitionist literature, which represented the negroes as a highly intelligent body, chafing under their yoke and eager to rise. He knew that the lonely Allegheny chain was a favorite route for escaping slaves, much used by the intrepid underground leaders of rescue work. He knew that in Jamaica and Guiana runaway blacks, the Maroons, had maintained impregnable settlements in upland valleys and plateaus not for decades but for generations, treating with the Crown officers as an independent power. Abolitionist literature was full of accounts of these heroic Maroons.

Once established in Harper's Ferry, he thought he could arm a large number of white and colored recruits from the arsenal. He could destroy or barricade the two bridges; taking hostages, he could use them in negotiating with attackers, and when ready, he could move forward. He later told one of the prisoners he took just why he chose Harper's Ferry: "I knew there were a great many guns there that would be of service to me, and if I could conquer Virginia, the balance of the Southern States would nearly conquer themselves, there being such a large number of slaves in them." One of his men, Jeremiah Anderson, wrote a brother late in September that they expected to win a victory at Harper's Ferry and push through Virginia and on southward, inciting the slaves to rise and carrying them forward in a growing body. When himself cap-

tured, Brown told Governor Wise that he had expected ample assistance once he put the ball in motion. From what States? asked
Wise. "From more than you'd believe if I should name them all,"
replied Brown, "but I *expected* more from Virginia, Tennessee, and
the Carolinas than from any others."

Here, perhaps, lay the paranoiac flaw in John Brown's mind, the
key to his type of reasoning insanity. On all subjects but one—
slavery and the possibility of ending it by a sudden stroke which
would provoke a broadening wave of slave uprisings as a rock
thrown into a pond sends forth widening ripples—he was sane. (An
admirer was later to call him the stone tossed by God into the black
pool of slavery.) He talked and acted with great coherence and
even acuteness; he laid ordinary plans rationally; he maintained
his domination over his followers, and was later to impress Governor Wise as exceptionally clear-headed and logical. But on this
special question of the readiness of slavery to crumble at a blow,
his monomania, as Amos A. Lawrence termed it, or his paranoia, as
a modern alienist would define it, rendered him irresponsible. This
it was that made him seem to some observers increasingly speculative and impulsive, a gambler on chance; from this paranoia, too,
sprang his sense of a God-given mission, in which Providence would
carry him to success even through seeming failure. When his confident blow met a sharp check, he was certain to grow confused.
Hence the conclusion of his ablest biographer that he seemed to
be losing the power of quick, effective decisions.

19

C. Vann Woodward (1960)

> *In his stimulating essay, "John Brown's Private War," C. Vann Woodward is more concerned with the reaction to the Harper's Ferry raid than with Brown himself. Skeptical about Brown's motives and ~ity, Woodward does credit the "wily old revolutionist" with shrewd handling of the Secret Six—his "fellow travelers"—and with being after the raid "a genius at self-justification." For Woodward, however, Brown's significance inheres not so much in his actions as in the meanings infused into his work by northern intellectuals and southern fire-eaters. Woodward views the intense responses evoked by Brown as the penultimate stage of the nation's plunge into disunion and war.[1]*

When news of the invasion was first flashed across the country, the most common reaction was that this was obviously the act of a madman, that John Brown was insane. This explanation was particularly attractive to Republican politicians and editors, whose party suffered the keenest embarrassment from the incident. Fall elections were on, and the new Congress was about to convene. Democrats immediately charged that John Brown's raid was the inevitable consequence of the "irresistible-conflict" and "higher-law" abolitionism preached by Republican leaders William H. Seward and Salmon P. Chase. "Brown's invasion," wrote Senator Henry Wilson of Massachusetts, "has thrown us, who were in a splendid position, into a defensive position. . . . If we are defeated next year we shall owe it to that foolish and insane movement of Brown's." The emphasis on insanity was taken up widely by Wilson's contemporaries and later adopted by historians.

---

[1] From C. Vann Woodward, "John Brown's Private War," in *The Burden of Southern History* (Baton Rouge: The Louisiana State University Press, 1968), pp. 45–49, 55–59, 66–68. Copyright © 1960, 1968 by The Louisiana State University Press, Inc. Reprinted by permission of The Louisiana State University Press.

It seems best to deal with the insanity question promptly, for it is likely to confuse the issue and cause us to miss the meaning of Harpers Ferry. In dealing with the problem it is important not to blink, as many of his biographers have done, at the evidence of John Brown's close association with insanity in both his heredity and his environment. In the Brown Papers at the Library of Congress are nineteen affidavits signed by relatives and friends attesting the record of insanity in the Brown family. John Brown's maternal grandmother and his mother both died insane. His three aunts and two uncles, sisters and brothers of his mother, were intermittently insane, and so was his only sister, her daughter, and one of his brothers. Of six first cousins, all more or less mad, two were deranged from time to time, two had been repeatedly committed to the state insane asylum, and two were still confined at the time. Of John Brown's immediate family, his first wife and one of his sons died insane, and a second son was insane at intervals. On these matters the affidavits, signers of which include Brown's uncle, a half brother, a brother-in-law, and three first cousins, are in substantial agreement. On the sanity of John Brown himself, however, opinion varied. Several believed that he was a "monomaniac," one that he was insane on subjects of religion and slavery, and an uncle thought his nephew had been "subject to periods of insanity" for twenty years.

The insurrectionist himself, of course, stoutly maintained that he was perfectly sane, and he was certainly able to convince many intelligent people, both friend and foe, that he was sane. He firmly refused to plead insanity at his trial. Governor Henry A. Wise of Virginia went so far as to write out orders to the superintendent of the state insane asylum to examine Brown, but endorsed the orders, "countermanded upon reflection." On the other hand, John Brown pronounced Governor Wise mad. "Hard to tell who's mad," jested Wendell Phillips to a laughing congregation in Henry Ward Beecher's church. "The world says one man's mad. John Brown said the same of the Governor. . . . I appeal from Philip drunk to Philip sober." He meant future generations when, he said, "the light of civilization has had more time to penetrate." Then it would be plain that not Brown but his enemies were mad.

We, the Philips sober of the future, with some misgiving about how far "the light of civilization" has penetrated, do think we know a little more about insanity than did our great-grandfathers. We at least know that it is a loose expression for a variety of mental disorders and that it is a relative term. What seems sane to some people at some times seems insane to other people at other times. In our own time we have witnessed what we consider psychopathic personalities rise to power over millions of people and plunge the world into war. Yet to the millions who followed them these leaders appeared sublime in their wisdom.

"John Brown may be a lunatic," observed the Boston *Post*, but if so, "then one-fourth of the people of Massachusetts are madmen," and perhaps three-fourths of the ministers of religion. Begging that Brown's life be spared, Amos A. Lawrence wrote Governor Wise: "Brown is a Puritan whose mind has become disordered by hardship and illness. He has the qualities wh. endear him to our people." The association of ideas was doubtless unintentional, but to the Virginian it must have seemed that Lawrence was saying that in New England a disordered mind was an endearing quality. The Reverend J. M. Manning of Old South Church, Boston, pronounced Harpers Ferry "an unlawful, a foolhardy, a suicidal act" and declared, "I stand before it wondering and admiring." Horace Greeley called it "the work of a madman" for which he had not "one reproachful word," and for the "grandeur and nobility" of which he was "reverently grateful." And the New York *Independent* declared that while "Harper's Ferry was insane, the controlling motive of this demonstration was sublime." It was both foolhardy and godly, insane and sublime, treasonous and admirable. . . .

The task to which the intellectuals of the cult dedicated themselves was the idealizing of John Brown as a symbol of the moral order and the social purpose of the Northern cause. Wendell Phillips expressed this best when he declared in the Boston Music Hall: " 'Law' and 'order' are only means for the halting ignorance of the last generation. John Brown is the impersonation of God's order and God's law, moulding a better future, and setting for it an example." In substituting the new revolutionary law and order for traditional law and order, the intellectuals encountered some tough problems in morals and values. It was essential for them to justify a code of political methods and morals that was at odds with the Anglo-American tradition.

John Brown's own solution to this problem was quite simple. It is set forth in the preamble of his Provisional Constitution of the United States, which declares that in reality slavery is an "unjustifiable War of one portion of its citizens upon another." War, in which all is fair, amounted to a suspension of ethical restraints.

This type of reasoning is identical with that of the revolutionaries who hold that class struggle is in reality a class war. The assumption naturally facilitates the justification of deeds otherwise indefensible. These might include the dissembling of motives, systematic deception, theft, murder, or the liquidation of an enemy class.

It is clear that certain enthusiasts found in Brown's reasoning a satisfactory solution to their moral problem, but it was equally clear that the mass of people were not yet ready to accept this solution and that some other rationalization was required. The doctrine of the "Higher Law" and the doctrine of "Civil Disobedience" had already done much to prepare the way for acceptance of the revolutionary ethics. They had justified conduct in defiance of the Constitution and the government by appeal to higher moral ends. Transcendental doctrine was now used to extend the defiance of tradition even further. Thoreau's reply to attacks upon John Brown's methods was: "The method is nothing; the spirit is all." This was the Transcendentalist way of saying that means are justified by the ends. According to this doctrine, if the end is sufficiently noble—as noble as the emancipation of the slave—any means used to attain the end is justified.

The crisis of Harpers Ferry was a crisis of means, not of ends. John Brown did not raise the question of whether slavery should be abolished or tolerated. That question had been raised in scores of ways and debated for a generation. Millions held strong convictions on the subject. Upon abolition, as an *end,* there was no difference between John Brown and the American and Foreign Anti-Slavery Society. But as to the *means* of attaining abolition, there was as much difference between them, so far as the record goes, as there is between the modern British Labour Party and the government of Soviet Russia on the means of abolishing capitalism. The Anti-Slavery Society was solemnly committed to the position of non-violent means. In the very petition that Lewis Tappan, secretary of the society, addressed to Governor Wise in behalf of Brown he repeated the rubric about "the use of all carnal weapons for deliverance from bondage." But in their rapture over Brown as martyr and saint the abolitionists lost sight of their differences with him over the point of means and ended by totally compromising their creed of nonviolence.

But what of those who clung to the democratic principle that differences should be settled by ballots and that the will of the majority should prevail? Phillips pointed out: "In God's world there are no majorities, no minorities; one, on God's side, is a majority." And Thoreau asked, "When were the good and the brave ever in a majority?" So much for majority rule. What of the issue of treason? The Reverend Fales H. Newhall of Roxbury declared that the word "treason" had been "made holy in the American language"; and the Reverend Edwin M. Wheelock of Boston blessed "the sacred, and the radiant 'treason' of John Brown."

No aversion to bloodshed seemed to impede the spread of the Brown cult. William Lloyd Garrison thought that "every slaveholder has forfeited his right to live" if he impeded emancipation. The Reverend Theodore Parker predicted a slave insurrection in which "The Fire of Vengeance" would run "from man to man, from town to town" through the South. "What shall put it out?" he asked. "The White Man's blood." The Reverend Mr. Wheelock thought Brown's "mission was to inaugurate slave insurrection as the divine weapon of the antislavery cause." He asked: "Do we shrink from the bloodshed that would follow?" and answered, "No such wrong [as slavery] was ever cleansed by rose-water." Rather than see slavery continued the Reverend George B. Cheever of New York declared: "It were infinitely better that three hundred thousand slaveholders were abolished, struck out of existence." In these pronouncements the doctrine that the end justifies the means had arrived pretty close to justifying the liquidation of an enemy class.

The reactions of the extremists have been stressed in part because it was the extremist view that eventually prevailed in the apotheosis of John Brown and, in part, because by this stage of the crisis each section tended to judge the other by the excesses of a few. "Republicans were all John Browns to the Southerners," as Professor Dwight L. Dumond has observed, "and slaveholders were all Simon Legrees to the Northerners." As a matter of fact Northern conservatives and unionists staged huge anti-Brown demonstrations that equaled or outdid those staged by the Brown partisans. Nathan Appleton wrote a Virginian: "I have never in my long life seen a fuller or more enthusiastic demonstration" than the anti-Brown meeting in Faneuil Hall in Boston. The Republican press described a similar meeting in New York as "the largest and most enthusiastic" ever held in that city. Northern politicians of high rank, including Lincoln, Douglas, Seward, Edward Everett, and Henry Wilson, spoke out against John Brown and his methods. The Republican party registered its official position by a plank in the 1860 platform denouncing the Harpers Ferry raid. Lincoln approved of Brown's execution, "even though he agreed with us in thinking slavery wrong." Agreement on ends did not mean agreement on means. "That cannot excuse violence, bloodshed, and treason," said Lincoln. . . .

Then there was the Southern enemy within the gates to be dealt with. Hinton R. Helper of North Carolina had written an antislavery book, quantities of which were burned in public ceremonies at High Point in his own state, at Greenville, South Carolina, and at Mayesville, Kentucky. Other public book-burning ceremonies took place at Enterprise, Mississippi, and at Montgomery, Alabama, while at Palestine, Texas, the citizens appointed a committee "to collect all said dangerous books for destruction by public burning." Thought control extended to the suppression and seizure of newspapers, a method long practiced, and in Alabama a resolution was introduced in the legislature prohibiting the licensing of teachers with less than ten years' residence, "to protect the state against abolition teachers." Not content with cutting off intellectual commerce with the North, extremists organized to end economic intercourse as well. They published blacklists of Northern firms suspected of abolitionist tendencies, organized boycotts, and promoted nonintercourse agreements. The Richmond *Enquirer* advocated a law "that will keep out of our borders every article of Northern manufacture or importation." On December 8, 1859, thirty-two business agents of New York and Boston arrived in Washington from the South, reporting "indignation so great against Northerners that they were compelled to return and abandon their business."

Southern zealots of secession had no better ally than John Brown. Robert B. Rhett, Edmund Ruffin, and William L. Yancey all rejoiced over the effect of Harpers Ferry. Non-slaveholders saw dramatized before them the menace of a slave uprising and readily concluded that their wives and children, as much as the home of the planter, were threatened with the horror of insurrection. They frequently became more fanatical secessionists than the planters. In face of the Northern apotheosis of Brown there was little that Southern moderates could say in answer to such pronouncements as that of the New Orleans *Picayune* of December 2: "Crime becomes godliness, and criminals, red from the slaughter of innocent, are exalted to eminence beside the divine gospel of Peace." The Charleston *Mercury* of November 29 rejoiced that Harpers Ferry, "like a slap in the face," had roused Virginia from her hesitant neutrality and started her on the road to secession. "I have never before seen the public mind of Va. so deeply moved," wrote a Virginian sadly. "The people are far in advance of the politicians, and would most cheerfully follow the extremist counsels. Volunteer companies, horse & foot, are springing up everywhere."

This crisis psychology of 1859 persisted and deepened in the fateful year of 1860 into a pathological condition of mind in which delusions of persecution and impending disaster flourished. Out of Texas came wild rumors of incendiary fires, abolitionists plotting with slaves, and impending insurrection on a vast scale. Rumors of large stocks of strychnine in the possession of slaves and of plans for well-poisoning were widely believed, though unproved. One scholar has aptly compared the tension of the South in 1860 with the "Great Fear" that seized the rural provinces of France in the summer of 1789 when panic spread the word that "the brigands are coming." In that atmosphere the South made the momentous decision that split the Democratic Party at Charleston in April, and before the mood was gone it was debating secession.

In the course of the crisis each of the antagonists, according to the immemorial pattern, had become convinced of the depravity and diabolism of the other. Each believed itself persecuted, menaced. "Let the 'higher law' of abolitionism be met by the 'higher law' of self-preservation," demanded the Richmond *Enquirer*. Lynch law was the only answer to pikes. "What additional insults and outrages *will* arouse it [the North] to assert its rights?" demanded Garrison. And Garrison's opposite number in Mississippi, Albert Gallatin Brown, cried: "Oh, God! To what depths of infamy are we sinking in the South if we allow these things to pass." Paranoia continued to induce counterparanoia, each antagonist infecting the other reciprocally, until the vicious spiral ended in war.

20

Benjamin Quarles (1969)

Benjamin Quarles writes about a neglected topic in American history, the black abolitionists. As he points out, the black abolitionist was not a camp follower in the anti-slavery movement but was its "different drummer," both a participant in and a symbol of the struggle against human bondage. Dealing with the men whom John Brown knew and worked with—Frederick Douglass, Martin Delany, Henry Highland Garnet, and Jermain Wesley Loguen—Quarles focuses on Brown's relationship with blacks and argues that Brown was uniquely free of the paternalistic condescension typical of many white abolitionists. His assessment that Brown's altruistic motivations and deep convictions sparked his involvement in the antislavery movement is in sharp contrast to Wilson's cynical assertion that the old man was driven solely by greed.[1]

The new climate of impending physical confrontation inevitably produced its own energizers. Of the abolitionist figures thrust up by the undercurrents of violence, one stands in a class by himself—John Brown of Osawatomie. To Brown, slavery itself was a species of warfare, demanding a counter resort to arms. Brown's daring sweep into Virginia in October 1859, his capture and his execution constituted a national shock from which there would be no recovery. Abolitionists hitherto of a pacifist orientation found reason to reverse themselves as the whole atmosphere became charged.

Brown's relationships with Negroes had been close, continuous, and on a peer basis, a pattern which no other white reformer could boast. Apparently no Negro who ever knew Brown ever said anything in criticism of his attitude or behavior toward colored peo-

[1] From *Black Abolitionists*, by Benjamin Quarles, pp. 235–45. Copyright © 1969 by Oxford University Press, Inc. Reprinted by permission. Footnotes omitted by permission of the author.

ple. Brown's attitude toward slavery and his grim and forceful response to it were shaped by many things, of which his own personal experiences with Negroes was not the least.

The reciprocal relations between John Brown and the blacks began long before five of them accompanied him to Harpers Ferry and four of them to his doom. Brown's interest in colored people dated back to 1834 when he proposed "to get at least one Negro boy or youth, and bring him up as we do our own." Fifteen years later Brown moved his family to North Elba, New York, expressly to settle among Negroes, most of them recipients of land grants from Gerrit Smith. Brown attempted to assist his Negro neighbors in business matters, and he invited them to his weekly sessions in the study of the Bible. Richard Henry Dana, paying a farewell call to John Brown at North Elba on a morning in late June 1849, noted that at the breakfast table eating with the family were the hired hands, including three Negroes.

Brown's attempt to spur Negroes on led him in 1848 to contribute a lengthy article to the *Ram's Horn,* a short-lived weekly. Entitled "Sambo's Mistakes," this article lampoons the habits of the Negro. Brown felt that the colored people were not doing all that they themselves could do in self-improvement. Hence in "Sambo's Mistakes" he makes his points by posing as a Negro who is offering to his fellows the benefit of his experience in life. A typical passage reads as follows:

> Another error of my riper years has been, that when any meeting of colored people has been called in order to consider any important matter of general interest, I have been so eager to display my spouting talents, and so tenacious of some trifling theory or other that I have adopted, that I have generally lost all sight of the business hand, consumed the time disputing about things of no moment, and thereby defeated entirely many important measures calculated to promote the general welfare; but I am happy to say I can see in a minute where I missed it.
>
> Another small error of my life (for I never committed great blunders) has been that I never would (for the sake of union in the furtherance of the most vital interests of our race) yield any minor point of difference. In this way I have always had to act with but a few, or more frequently alone, and could accomplish nothing worth living for; but I have one comfort, I can see in a minute where I missed it.

If few men knew the Negro's shortcomings as perceptively as Brown, there were even fewer who were as distressed by color prejudice as he. One of his followers relates that while walking in Boston in April 1857 Brown was greatly annoyed at the rude language addressed to a colored girl, language of the type, Brown said, that would not have been directed to a white girl. Entering the Massasoit House in Chicago for breakfast on April 25, 1858, Brown was told that the Negro member of his party, Richard Richardson, a fugitive slave, could not be served. Brown marched out, although not before subjecting the proprietor to "a little bit of terse logic."

Aside from his equalitarian principles, Brown was interested in the welfare of the colored people because he had something for them to do. His all-consuming passion was the abolition of slavery, an end which he proposed to accomplish by enlisting a semi-militaristic group of followers ready for direct action. Brown's role for the Negro was implicit in an organization he formed in January 1851 at Springfield, Massachusetts, the United States League of Gileadites. Formed to resist the Fugitive Slave Law, the Gileadites pledged themselves to go armed and to shoot to kill, a pattern of conduct that would characterize Brown's later operations in Kansas and at Harpers Ferry. The forty-four colored men and women who signed the agreement apparently had little call for action. Moreover, in March 1851, Brown, the original man-in-motion, left for Ohio.

Brown was interested in recruiting Negro leaders and the black rank and file. Prominent figures sought out by Brown included Frederick Douglass, Martin R. Delany, Stephen Smith, Jermain W. Loguen, Henry Highland Garnet, William Still, and Charles H. Langston. His contacts with Douglass, whom he desperately wished to win over, stretched over a longer time-span and were more numerous than with any other Negro leader. Brown's acquaintance with Douglass went back to the spring of 1848 when the latter, at Brown's request, visited him at Springfield. In the spring of 1858 Brown paid two visits to the Douglass home in Rochester, New York, one of them extending over a period of two weeks. While a guest of Douglass, Brown met a fugitive slave, Shields Green, who would accompany him to Harpers Ferry.

Shortly before Brown got ready to make his raid into Virginia he arranged to meet Douglass at Chambersburg, Pennsylvania, some twenty miles from the site of the planned foray. Douglass brought a letter for Brown from Mrs. J. N. Gloucester, a Brooklyn woman of means, with $25 enclosed. Douglass was accompanied by Shields

Green, the two of them being led to Brown's hideout by Harry Watson, a Negro underground railroad operator at Chambersburg. For three days Brown tried to persuade Douglass to join the expedition. Douglass steadfastly refused, discretion having formed his decision.

Not a single other Negro leader would join Brown, all of them considering his venture imprudent. On May 17, 1859, Brown wrote to Loguen: "I will just whisper in your private ear that I have no doubt you will soon have a call from God to minister at a different location." Despite the language, the Negro clergyman remained unconvinced. Loguen, like other Negroes, admired Brown for his antislavery exploits in Kansas and his daring excursion into Missouri in which he had freed eleven slaves by a show of force. However, as much as they revered Brown for his courage, Negro leaders thought that the proposed seizure of Harpers Ferry was inordinately risky, if not foolhardy.

Brown's most ambitious attempt to enlist the Negro rank and file was the holding of a convention at Chatham, Ontario, in early May, 1858. Brown's own party of twelve was present, as were thirty-four Negroes. These included the presiding officer, a Negro clergyman, William C. Munroe, the poet James Madison Bell, and Martin R. Delany, the last named then practicing medicine at Chatham, having come at the urgent personal invitation of Brown himself. The chief work of the convention was the adoption of a provisional constitution of the United States, a document which avowed the Declaration of Independence and condemned slavery.

The Chatham convention lacked follow-up. With Brown gone and with no action of any kind forthcoming for more nearly seventeen months, the enthusiasm of the Chatham signers abated, never to be rekindled. But at Chatham, Brown for the first time had met Harriet Tubman. He had thought of her as the shepherd of the slaves that he would shake loose. Brown's tête-à-tête with Harriet confirmed his already high opinion of her. But neither she nor Delany would be with him at Harpers Ferry. Brown, however, had not left Chatham empty-handed. A young printer's devil, Osborn Perry Anderson, had been impressed by the convention and by its convener; he would be the only black survivor of Harpers Ferry.

By the autumn of 1859 Brown was ready to seize the government arsenal at Harpers Ferry, a prelude to establishing a stronghold in the mountains and thus liberating the slaves on a mounting scale of operations. Late in the night of October 16 Brown moved into the town, leaving three of his party at the Kennedy Farm, the base of operations in Maryland. Marching into the darkened Harpers Ferry behind Brown were eighteen followers, five of them Negroes, Osborn Perry Anderson, Shields Green, Dangerfield Newby, like Green an escaped slave, and two recruits from Oberlin, Ohio—John A. Copeland, Jr., and Lewis S. Leary, his uncle. Copeland, a former student in the preparatory department at Oberlin College and the most articulate of the five, had joined Brown "to assist in giving that freedom to at least a few of my poor and enslaved brethren who have been most foully and unjustly deprived of their liberty."

John Brown was hardly a battlefield tactician; lacking a clear and definite plan of campaign, his raid was quickly suppressed. The first of the five fatalities inflicted by Brown's men was on a free Negro, Heywood Shepherd, baggage master of the train depot, a contretemps which seemed to set the stage for a military fiasco. Ten of Brown's band were killed, Newby first and Leary later. Copeland and Green were among the seven who were captured, and Anderson was among the five who escaped.

Brown and his captured followers were imprisoned in Charleston. Brown was tried first, and on October 31 the jury returned with a verdict of guilty. Two days later the judge pronounced a sentence of death by hanging. During the thirty-day interval between the sentence and the execution, Brown bore himself with fortitude and serenity.

Brown's inner peace was not shared by his countrymen, particularly those in the North. For his act, however rash and wrongheaded, had dramatized the issue of slavery, forcing neutrals to abandon their fence-sitting posture and giving to the abolitionists a martyr figure of unprecedented proportions. Charles H. Langston, like half a dozen white abolitionists, felt the necessity of issuing a "card of denial" stating that he had had no hand in the Harpers Ferry affair. "But what shall I deny," added Langston. "I cannot deny that I feel the very deepest sympathy with the immortal John Brown in his heroic and daring effort to free the slaves." Langston's sentiment of sympathy and esteem mirrored the reaction of the overwhelming majority of black Americans.

During Brown's month in jail innumerable prayer and sympathy meetings were held throughout the North. None were more fervent than those called by Negroes. *The Weekly Anglo-African* for November 5 carried a guest editorial by James W. C. Pennington entitled, "Pray for John Brown." Such advice was hardly needed. On the day after Brown was sentenced a group of Providence Negroes, meeting at the Zion Church, expressed their full sympathy for Captain John Brown. Despite their "abhorrence to bloodshed and civil war," they referred to Brown, as "hero, philanthropist and unflinching champion of liberty," and pledged themselves to send up their prayers to Almighty God on his behalf. A group of Chicago Negroes, meeting later that month, drafted a letter to Brown assuring him of their deep sympathy and their intention to contribute material aid to his family: "How could we be so ungrateful as to do less for one who has suffered, bled, and now ready to die for the cause?" At the Siloam Presbyterian Church in Brooklyn, a prayer meeting cutting across denominational lines was led by the pastor, A. N. Freeman, assisted by fellow clergymen Henry Highland Garnet, James N. Gloucester, and Amos G. Beman.

Colored women sent letters of esteem to the jailed Brown. A group of Brooklyn matrons wrote that they would ever hold him in their remembrance, considering him a model of true patriotism because he sacrificed everything for his country's sake. From Kendalville, Indiana, Frances Ellen Watkins sent a letter on behalf of the slave women, an admixture of Christian faith in the future and symbolic references to the past—"You have rocked the bloody Bastile," and, "The hemlock is distilled with victory when it is pressed to the lips of Socrates." A group of women from New York, Brooklyn, and Williamsburg sent Mrs. Brown a letter on November 23, its content summarized in the lines, "Fear not, beloved sister. Trust in the God of Jacob."

As John Brown stepped from the jail on the last morning of his life, "no little slave-child was held up for the benison of his lips, for none but soldiers were near and the street was full of marching men." However, as Brown was led to the gallows, a slave woman said, "God bless you, old man; if I could help you, I would." Brown went to his death with dignity, and the day concluded, wrote one who was present, "with the calm & quiet of a New England Sabbath."

If December 2, 1859, was also a quiet day in abolitionist circles, it was due to the nature of its observance. Throughout the North reformers held prayer meetings or meetings with a religious orientation. At Boston, where all Negro businesses were closed, the colored people, wearing arm bands of black crepe, held three prayer meetings—morning, afternoon, and night—at Leonard Grimes's Twelfth Baptist Church. Many persons stayed from one meeting to the next, not needing to go out for meals on a day of widespread fasting. One of these all-day sojourners was Lydia Maria Child, who had journeyed from Wayland, fifteen miles away, to spend the solemn day with Negroes. She therefore had to miss the much larger meeting at Tremont Temple arranged by the white abolitionists but with Negroes attending in large numbers and with J. Sella Martin as one of the featured speakers. But perhaps it was just as well that Mrs. Child did not go to the crowded Temple, for thousands were turned away.

Martyr Day, as some black abolitionists called it, was appropriately observed by New York Negroes at a meeting at Shiloh Church beginning at ten in the morning and with a period of silent prayer at noon. Of the six clergymen on the program, William Goodell, the only white speaker, differed from two of his colleagues on one point. When James N. Gloucester endorsed John Brown's course, Goodell dissented on the grounds that the weapons of the abolitionists were moral and religious rather than carnal. Sampson White took issue, informing Goodell that George Washington, whom Americans revered, had not taken the position that "our weapons are not carnal" when he led the new nation in its struggle against English oppression. Washington and the Americans of his day had acted on the premise that "resistance to tyrants was obedience to God." White, somewhat carried away, said that he had an arm which he felt duty-bound to use when his God-given rights were invaded.

Philadelphia Negroes, like those in Boston, observed Martyr Day by closing down their businesses. Public prayer meetings were held at two churches—Shiloh and Union Baptist. Hundreds of colored men and women went to National Hall to hear Robert Purvis and white William Furness. Pittsburgh's black community held a meeting addressed by native son George Vashon. At Detroit the colored people gathered at the Second Baptist Church where they passed a resolution vowing to venerate Brown's character, regarding him as "our temporal leader whose name will never die."

On Martyr Day at Cleveland the two thousand who managed to get into crowded Melodeon Hall included almost as many whites as blacks, with almost as many equally mixed milling around outside, unable to get in. Judges and members of the state legislature were among the platform guests flanking the presiding officer, Charles H. Langston. The walls were draped in black and the stage was hung with large-lettered, framed quotations from John Brown's writings and conversations. Negroes in lesser towns throughout the North—from Worcester, Massachusetts, to Galesburg, Ohio—likewise paused on December 2, 1859, to honor John Brown on the day of his death.

Negroes felt that they had an especial obligation to assist in the efforts to give financial aid to John Brown's widow. Their donations would not be large, but they would represent a more widespread giving than their modest totals might indicate. The John Brown Relief Fund of New Haven raised $12.75 for Mary Brown. Philadelphia Negroes sent her $150 and the recently formed John Brown Liberty League of Detroit donated $25. Some Negroes, such as Frances Ellen Watkins, sent personal contributions. Mrs. Brown's letters of acknowledgement were brief, but gracious and inspirational.

The sympathy that Negroes felt for Mrs. Brown extended to Mrs. Mary Leary, widow of Lewis S. Leary. The wife and seven children of the other Negro who fell at Harpers Ferry, Dangerfield Newby, were in slavery, and neither of the two Negroes who were hanged, John A. Copeland or Shields Green, was married. Boston Negroes raised $40 for Mrs. Leary and her child, and $10 to go toward erecting a mounment to the memory of the heroes of Harpers Ferry. The colored women in Brooklyn and New York sent Mrs. Leary a total of $140, bringing from her the reply that her loss had been great but she hoped that her husband and his associates had not died in vain in their "attack on that great evil—American Slavery."

Negroes did not wait for history to pass the verdict on John Brown. He was the greatest man of the nineteenth century, ran a resolution adopted by a group of New Bedford Negroes two days after he mounted the scaffold. This evaluation was echoed by Frederick Douglass in a letter to Brown's associate, James Redpath, on June 29, 1860. Brown's portrait graced the wall of the Purvis diningroom at Byberry, Pennsylvania; in Troy, New York, the black childred pooled their pennies so that they might buy a picture of him for their school. A Negro weekly compared him with Nat Turner, discovering that both were idealistic, Bible-nurtured, tenacious of purpose, swayed by spiritual impulses, and calm and heroic in prison.

The evaluation of Brown by Negroes was uncritical, since he perhaps "was worth more for hanging than anything else." But as prophets, Negroes did better. For with the ensuing rapid current of national events Brown's fate became a rallying cry and his name a legend. It is true, wrote John A. Copeland, as he sat in the jail awaiting the hangman's noose, that the outbreak at Harpers Ferry did not give immediate freedom to the slave but it was the prelude to that event.

21

Stephen B. Oates (1970)

Stephen B. Oates's recent biography of John Brown, based on prodigious research, uses both traditional and newly uncovered evidence to present a complete picture of the life of its subject. Offering subtle corrections of fact and chronology to Villard's narrative, Oates provides the most accurate, complete, and objective treatment of Brown yet written. Although empathetic with his subject, Oates confronts directly the undistinguished and sometimes indefensible aspects of Brown's first fifty-five years, concealing none of the seamy details. Nevertheless, he concludes that the Harper's Ferry raid earned Brown a prominent place in history. Oates's insight into Brown's personality development is the most sophisticated analysis attempted by any historian of Brown.[1]

Meanwhile Brown's own lawyers made a last desperate attempt to save his life. In November Hoyt visited Washington and talked with Montgomery Blair, a Missouri Republican who was convinced that Southern fire-eaters would use Harpers Ferry to break up the Union. Anxious to block their efforts Blair suggested that "a demonstration of Brown's insanity might please Wise," that the governor might be willing to commit Brown to an asylum. Blair thought that if Brown could be presented to the divided nation as a "lunatic" who had perpetrated an "insane act," it might quell the sectional storm which Harpers Ferry had provoked.

Inspired by Blair's suggestion, Hoyt traveled to Ohio and collected affidavits regarding Brown's "insanity" from nineteen of his relatives and friends, who were anxious indeed to save him from the gallows. Among the affiants were Jeremiah Brown, a half brother; Sylvester Thompson and Gideon Mills, relatives on his

[1] From pp. 329–34 in *To Purge This Land With Blood: A Biography of John Brown* by Stephen B. Oates, Copyright © 1970 by Stephen B. Oates. Reprinted by permission of Harper & Row, Publishers, Inc. Footnotes have been omitted.

mother's side; Milton Lusk, Dianthe's brother (who had never liked Brown but did not want him to hang either); and old friends like Orson M. Oviatt, George Leach, and Edwin Wetmore. To begin with, many of the affiants claimed that "insanity" ran in the maternal side of Brown's family and that Brown himself was "laboring under hereditary insanity." Thompson and others asserted that Brown's grandmother (Ruth Humphrey Mills) was "said to be insane" during the last six years of her life. Contrary to what several writers have claimed, there were no references made to any mental trouble on the part of Brown's mother, Ruth Mills Brown. But one or two of her brothers and three of her sisters—Thompson's mother, Susan Richardson, and Sarah Woodruff—were alleged to have been "insane." Three of Gideon Mills's children and two children of Oliver Mills were "intermittently insane." Brown's "only sister" and his brother Salmon were "thought to be at times insane." Other cousins and relatives of Brown's on his mother's side had shown symptoms. The affiants also pointed out that Brown's wife Dianthe had been "afflicted" and so had two of her sons—John Jr. and Frederick.

As for Brown himself, the affidavits varied as to the degree and nature of his "mental derangement." Many of the affiants stated that, while Brown was "an honest," "deeply religious," "very conscientious" man, he had always had an "excitable mind" when it came to religious matters and slavery. Milton Lusk and Sylvester Thompson both claimed that Brown's behavior had been "erratic" and "peculiar" after he moved from Pennsylvania back to Ohio in 1835. Lusk (who mentioned nothing about his sister's troubles) argued that Brown had been "more or less insane" since shortly after Dianthe's death. His penchant "for wild & desperate projects" was proof that he had "an unsound mind." George Leach, who had known Brown from boyhood, contended that Brown had been "a monomaniac" in some of his business affairs in Ohio. S. Goodale agreed. "I have known John Brown for 15 years," Goodale testified, "and never saw any business transaction conducted by him which indicated a Sane mind—excepting while engaged in Summit County in growing sheep & wool." Brown's wool crusade in Springfield, Goodale argued, showed that Brown was "clearly insane." Jonathan Metcalf, a seventy-two-year-old physician of Hudson, had always thought Brown subject to "fits of insecurity" and at times "completely insane." Metcalf had talked with Brown in 1855, when he was on his way to Kansas, and thought him "fanatically insane" on the subject of slavery. (It would be instructive to know the physician's opinions about slavery, just to keep the record straight.) Metcalf's wife had known Brown's grandmother, and the doctor had "heard her say" that the grandmother was "insane"—although Metcalf admitted that he had no "personal knowledge of this fact." Several of the other affiants believed that it was the horror Brown had experienced in Kansas that had caused his mind to become "deranged." Jeremiah Brown had seen the old man in 1857 and recalled how he spoke obsessively about his mission to free the slaves. William Otis, who had known Brown at Ravenna and Akron, said that Brown had long suffered from "religious fixations" and that after Kansas he had become a "monomaniac" on the subject of slavery. Otis concluded this from two conversations he'd had with Brown "after his return from Kansas." David L. King of Akron said he had talked with Brown in April, 1859, and had also decided that "on the subject of slavery he was crazy—he was armed to the teeth & remarked among other things that he was an 'instrument in the hands of God to free the slaves.'" Other affiants thought that the fighting in Kansas combined with the loss of Frederick and a lifetime of sickness and hardship had "deranged his mind." Gideon Mills, who thought Brown had been of unsound mind for twenty years, was frankly shocked at Brown's invasion of Virginia. Mills had thought Brown's "insanity" was "harmless." He never dreamed it would lead Brown to Harpers Ferry.

Since many writers have accepted these affidavits at face value and have used them as proof that Brown was a "madman" out of touch with "reality," the documents—and the whole insanity question—merit careful examination. To begin with, the word "insanity" is a vague, emotion-charged, and clinically meaningless term. Modern psychology has long since abandoned it in describing mental and emotional disorders. And historians should abandon it as well. As C. Vann Woodward has reminded us, the term even in historical context is misleading, ambiguous, and relative—it has meant different things to different peoples in the past, and what seems "insane" in one period of time may seem perfectly "sane" at other times. Even in nineteenth-century parlance, "insanity" was a catchall term used to describe a wide range of odd or unacceptable behavior, including epilepsy and multiple sclerosis. Consequently, when Brown's relatives and friends talk about instances of "insanity" in the family, we do not know what sort of disorders they were describing. Maybe some of the cases were epileptics or mentally retarded.

The whole argument about Brown's alleged "hereditary insanity" is open to dispute. Modern psychologists themselves do not agree on how much of the human personality is inherited (if any of it is) and how much is the result of the environment. Any biographer or historian who argues that "insanity" is hereditary intrudes upon his craft the controversies and disagreements of what is still an imprecise science. And even if one persists in arguing that Brown labored from "hereditary insanity," one must rest one's case on the assumption that his disorders came from his grandmother. And there is no evidence at all as to what her trouble was. Maybe she was just senile.

Historians have described "the instances of insanity" in Brown's family as "a fearful record." But in truth the record is more fearful for the Mills and Thompson sides of the family than for the Browns. Probably it did not occur to Gideon Mills or Sylvester Thompson, as they testified to the "insanity" of their mothers, their aunts and uncles, and Mills's own children, that they might be raising far more serious questions about their own mental health than about John Brown's—*if* one accepts the moot argument that emotional and mental disorders can be inherited at all.

In the case of Brown's immediate family, the affidavits contained a great deal of information based not on direct knowledge of the condition of Brown's sister and his brother Salmon but on hearsay (as Sylvester Thompson admitted). In fact, there is no evidence that Salmon, who was editor of the New Orleans *Bee* and a prominent lawyer of that city, was "insane." As for Brown's sons (Frederick and John Jr.), if one accepts the assumption that "mental aberrations" are hereditary, then one must face the argument that both sons inherited their "troubles" from Dianthe, not from Brown. Actually a much more plausible explanation is that John Jr.'s depression and melancholia resulted from his experiences in Kansas: the constant haggling with his father as to what they should do during the Lawrence crisis, the tension and lack of sleep, the humiliation he had suffered when his friends turned against him after the Pottawatomie massacre, and the cruel treatment he received at the hands of U.S. troops following his capture. And what of Frederick? If we may believe Samuel Adair, Frederick was suffering from what doctors at that time diagnosed as "an accumulation of blood on the brain" that caused "blinding headaches" and occasionally left him "flighty" and incoherent. He could have had a brain tumor. Or perhaps his trouble was epilepsy.

Finally—and this is a crucial point—the affidavits Hoyt collected in Ohio were intended first and foremost to save Brown's life, by convincing Governor Wise and the state of Virginia that Brown was "insane," that he was not responsible for his acts, and that he should be placed in an asylum. The documents were not objective clinical evidence gathered by doctors who wanted to establish as clearly as possible what Brown's "mental disorders" were. When the affiants asserted that Brown was "insane," they were giving their opinions for a partisan objective. And, although many of them doubtless believed their opinions were true, they were still opinions. Except for Dr. Metcalf, none of the affiants were educated in medical matters and none of them were psychologists.

All this is not to argue that Brown was a "normal," "well-adjusted," "sane" individual. These terms are meaningless too. That he was a revolutionary who believed himself called by God to a special destiny (a notion that stemmed from his Calvinist beliefs), that he had an excitable temperament and could get carried away with one idea, that he was inept, egotistical, hard on his sons, afflicted with chronic attacks of the ague, worn down from a lifetime of hardship, and enraged enough at his "slave-cursed" country to contemplate destroying it, that he could have five men he regarded as his enemies assassinated in cold blood (after proslavery forces had murdered six free-state men in cold blood), and that he wanted to become either an American Spartacus at the head of a slave army or a martyred soldier who was the first to die in a sectional war over slavery—all this is true. Yet to dismiss Brown as an "insane" man is to ignore the tremendous sympathy he felt for the suffering of the black man in the United States; it is to disregard the fact that at a time when most Northerners and almost all Southerners were racists who wanted to keep the Negro at the bottom of society, John Brown was able to treat America's "poor despised Africans" as fellow human beings. And to label him a "maniac" out of touch with "reality" is to ignore the piercing insight he had into what his raid—whether it succeeded or whether it failed—would do to sectional tensions that already existed between North and South. Nor can John Brown be removed from the violent, irrational, and paradoxical times in which he lived. A man of "powerful religious convictions" who believed to his bones that slavery was "a sin against God," he was profoundly disturbed that a nation which claimed to be both Christian and free should condone, protect, and perpetuate that "sum of villanies." It was not only Brown's angry, messianic mind, but the racist, slave society in which he lived—one that professed "under God" to provide liberty and justice for all—that helped bring John Brown to Harpers Ferry.

"John Brown may be a lunatic," the Boston *Post* declared, but if so "then one-fourth of the people of Massachusetts are madmen" and three-fourths of the ministers of the gospel. At a time when thousands of Northerners remained indifferent to the contradiction of slavery in a self-proclaimed "free and just" Republic, at a time when Christians, scientists, and politicians (in North and South alike) heralded Negro slavery as "enlightened" and "inevitable," at a time when thousands of Southerners were plagued with fears of a Black Republican invasion and haunted by nightmares of Negro rebels raping "our wives and daughters," it was indeed (as Wendell Phillips said) "Hard to tell who's mad."

Afterword

John Brown was, at the very least, a singularly remarkable man. He raised himself out of a life of obscurity and frustration by his single-minded devotion to a cause. He not only refused to ignore the central issue of his day, but he attacked that issue frontally and righteously. As a result, John Brown was transformed from man to symbol. For some, whose efforts Brown so willingly assisted in his letters from the Charlestown jail, he became a martyr saint in the cause of abolitionism; for others, whose fears Brown may have relished, he represented a fanatical devil in the crisis of sectional conflict. In either case, practically all his contemporaries agreed with Herman Melville that "Weird" John Brown was "The Portent," "The meteor of the war."

John Brown's life can be considered great only because of Harper's Ferry. While men like William Lloyd Garrison chose to agitate the slavery question, Brown chose to attack the slavery system. Where Henry David Thoreau stood on principle and committed civil disobedience, Brown committed treason. In assessing his convictions and actions and in reviewing the responses to him and his deed, one can comprehend fully the explosive and desperate state of the nation in 1859. That Brown conceived and executed his raid, that responsible men were prepared to back him in such a venture, and that men of all persuasions should react so violently to the Harper's Ferry incident—all these are clear signs that the nation was on the verge of division. John Brown did not cause that division, he dramatized it. He represented the penultimate moment before the Civil War when violent rhetoric gave way to physical violence.

Nevertheless, John Brown's place in the American heritage is ambivalent. The scores of books about him and the raid testify that he has not suffered neglect from historians. But the historical works and interpretive debates have been overshadowed in the popular mind by two famous renditions of the man: the Civil War marching song, "John Brown's Body," and Stephen Vincent Benet's epic poem of the same title. For most Americans, John Brown is a folk hero of sorts, a romantic, quixotic figure from the past whose "great work" is unknown or misunderstood and whose divisive role is almost forgotten.

Anyone who confronts John Brown first-hand in the context of his times can no longer hold to such a picture. His legacy is larger than song and legend. His later life represents, quite simply, a challenge to the process of orderly and legal remedies to social ills and a response to the failure of such remedies to effect change. When legal solutions fail to meet widely perceived needs, when civil disobedience fails to alter policy, acts of violence often result. In the American experience, such acts have served periodically to crystallize the tensions and fears in the national mood. John Brown's raid on Harper's Ferry stands with the Boston Massacre, the Nat Turner insurrection, the Haymarket Riot, Watts, and the killings at Kent State as occasions for the country to clarify—and even polarize—its major concerns. This, for better or for worse, is part of the legacy of John Brown.

Another is that he and Harper's Ferry were in fact and represent in theory the kind of man and event engendered by national despair. They could only come together in a time of turmoil. It is not surprising, therefore, that Brown's memory should be revived at similar moments. Malcolm X did so most recently when in 1965 he advised young white liberals: "If you are for me and my problems—when I say *me,* I mean us, our people—then you have to be willing to do as old John Brown did." John Brown embodies, then, the actual despair of his own time and the potential despair of all times. He is a watchword and a warning that when a nation fails to resolve its problems and allows them to reach crisis proportions—particularly those that threaten human rights and liberties—the response of a John Brown is possible and often inevitable.

There is, however, a further legacy of John Brown. He was, in his last years especially, a man of purpose who translated thought to action, who attempted what others only contemplated, and who was faithful to the dictates of his conscience. John Brown believed in the promise of the Declaration of Independence and anguished over its unfulfillment. However one may judge his means, he sought to realize that promise for black Americans. He dreamed of the more perfect Union that would not come until, as he predicted, the crimes of this guilty land were purged away with blood.

Bibliographical Note

Readers wishing to supplement the primary materials included in this volume may find additional sources in other printed works. The richest selection of Brown's letters is in Franklin B. Sanborn's pro-Brown biography, *The Life and Letters of John Brown* (Boston: Roberts Brothers, 1891). Richard J. Hinton's *John Brown and His Men* (New York: Funk & Wagnalls Company, 1894) includes a number of contemporary accounts of Brown and his raiding party as well as documents written by Brown himself. *The Report of the Select Committee of the Senate Appointed to Inquire into the Late Invasion and Seizure of the Public Property at Harper's Ferry*, Report Com. No. 278, 36th Congress, 1st Session (Washington, D.C., 1860) not only contains the findings and testimony of the so-called "Mason Report" but also includes transcripts of some of the materials recovered in Brown's satchel after the raid. The most complete account of the raid and trial can be found in *The Life, Trial, and Execution of John Brown* (New York: Robert W. DeWitt, 1859). James Redpath collected favorable northern responses to Brown and the raid in *Echoes of Harper's Ferry* (Boston: Thayer and Eldridge, 1860); included in Redpath's collection is Henry David Thoreau's famous "A Plea for Captain John Brown," which is currently available in several recent editions of Thoreau's writings. *The Virginia Magazine of History and Biography, 10–11* (July 1902—July 1903) reprinted many of the letters that poured in to Governor Wise and others in the aftermath of the raid. Two recent anthologies, Louis Ruchames, ed., *John Brown: The Making of a Revolutionary* (New York: Grosset & Dunlap, 1969) and Richard Scheidenhelm, ed., *The Responses to John Brown* (Belmont, California: Wadsworth Publishing Company, Inc., 1972) contain useful primary material by and about Brown. Finally, Oswald Garrison Villard quoted extensively from primary sources in *John Brown, 1800–1859: A Biography Fifty Years After* (Boston: Houghton, Mifflin, and Company, 1910). Of the volumes mentioned above, those by Sanborn, Hinton, Redpath, and Villard, as well as *The Life, Trial, and Execution of John Brown*, have recently been reissued.

Several manuscript collections are invaluable for a study of John Brown and Harper's Ferry. The most extensive one is owned by Boyd B. Stutler of Charleston, West Virginia, and is available on microfilm. Also on microfilm are John Brown's journal and memorandum book, which are in the Boston Public Library. The Thomas Wentworth Higginson Papers, also in the Boston Public Library, contain many items that shed light on the

activities of the Secret Six. The Sanborn Folder in the Houghton Library
at Harvard University is especially complete in its collection of Brown's
early correspondence. The John Brown Papers and the papers of Virginia
Governor Henry A. Wise, both in the Library of Congress, include valuable
material on the post-raid period; the Wise Papers contain the insanity
depositions collected as part of Brown's appeal attempt.

The Harper's Ferry raid was a sensational event which attracted extensive newspaper coverage. The editorials of a range of newspapers offer a
vivid account of the diversity of political, geographical, and ideological
responses to Brown. The best reportage of the raid, trial, and immediate
impact of John Brown can be found in The *New York Times,* The *New
York Daily Tribune,* and The *Baltimore American and Commercial Advertiser.* For further examples of editorial reactions, see almost any major
city newspaper; most of these are available on microfilm. The *Congressional Globe,* which reprinted the Senate debate over the creation of the
"Mason Committee," is the best single source of political responses to
Brown.

There are countless numbers of secondary works and articles about
Brown. In addition to the books excerpted in Part Three, a few others
deserve mention: W. E. B. DuBois, *John Brown* (Philadelphia: George W.
Jacobs & Company, 1909) presents a favorable view of Brown and stresses
his willingness to work with black men, not simply for them; Robert Penn
Warren, *John Brown: The Making of a Martyr* (New York: Payson &
Clarke, Ltd., 1929) offers a pro-South indictment of Brown. Stephen B.
Oates's *To Purge This Land With Blood* (New York: Harper & Row,
Publishers, 1970) is not only the best scholarly treatment of the man but
also proved to be the first of a group of works in a recent John Brown
renaissance. Following this book came Jules C. Abels, *Man on Fire: John
Brown and the Cause of Liberty* (New York: The Macmillan Company,
1971), Nelson Truman, *The Old Man: John Brown at Harper's Ferry*
(New York: Holt, Rinehart & Winston, Inc., 1972), and Richard O. Boyer,
The Legend of John Brown: A Biography and a History (New York: Alfred A. Knopf, Inc., 1973).

Several books deal effectively with portions of Brown's career. The best
of these is James C. Malin's *John Brown and the Legend of Fifty-Six*
(Philadelphia: The American Philosophical Society, 1942), which is a
full and critical examination of Brown's exploits in Kansas. Joseph C.
Furnas, *The Road to Harper's Ferry* (New York: W. Sloane Associates,
1959) deals primarily with the involvement of the Secret Six in the planning of the raid. Richard Morris presents a stimulating analysis of the
trial in a chapter entitled "The Treason Trial of John Brown" in his
book *Fair Trial* (New York: Alfred A. Knopf, Inc., 1952).

For a discussion of the creation of the song "John Brown's Body," see
Boyd B. Stutler, "John Brown's Body," in *Civil War History, 4* (Septem-

ber, 1958), 251–60. The origins of the legend concerning Brown kissing a slave mother's child on the way to the gallows are discussed in Cecil D. Eby, Jr., "Whittier's 'Brown of Ossawatomie,'" *The New England Quarterly, 33* (December, 1969), 452–61. The most famous literary creation inspired by Brown is, of course, Stephen Vincent Benet's *John Brown's Body* (Garden City, New York: Doubleday, Doran & Co., 1928). A recent dramatization based on Brown's raid is the play *Harpers Ferry* by Barrie Stavis (Cranbury, New Jersey: A. S. Barnes and Co., 1967).

There are a number of books that provide an overview of the period and issues relative to the study of John Brown. Allan Nevins's *The Emergence of Lincoln,* 2 vols. (New York: Charles Scribner's Sons, 1950) is one of the best. Roy F. Nichols gives a good account of the political history of the 1850s in *The Disruption of American Democracy* (New York: Macmillan Co., 1948), and David Brion Davis offers a rich analysis of the climate of opinion in which Brown's raid was interpreted in *The Slave Power Conspiracy and the Paranoid Style* (Baton Rouge, Louisiana: Louisiana State University Press, 1970). Steven A. Channing's *Crisis of Fear* (New York: Simon and Schuster, 1970) contains interesting sections on the southern reaction to the raid. Among several fine studies of the abolitionist movement, see: Gilbert H. Barnes, *The Antislavery Impulse* (New York: D. Appleton–Century Co., 1933), and Dwight L. Dumond, *Antislavery* (Ann Arbor: Michigan University Press, 1961).

Index

A

Alcott, Bronson, 15, 150
Anderson, Jeremiah, 153
Anderson, Osborn, 43, 165–66
Avis, Capt. John, 90, 92, 102–3

B

Beecher, Henry Ward, 104–7, 156
Benét, Stephen Vincent, 177
Black Jack, battle of, 10, 78
Blair, Charles, 15, 31, 59
Blair, Montgomery, 85, 171
Botts, Lawson, 81, 85
Brown, John:
  aliases of, 11, 15, 35, 63
  business ventures, 2–5
  early life, 1–5, 20–25, 111
  execution, 16, 102–3, 125–26
  Kansas experiences, 8–11, 13, 15,
    26–30, 66, 90, 105–6, 121–22,
    137, 147–48, 151
  Missouri raid, 15, 53, 72, 82, 151–
    52
  personality, 2–5, 20–25, 111, 124,
    136–38, 146–48
  religious views, 1–2, 4, 8, 10, 13,
    24, 73, 89–102
  sanity, 81–82, 85–87, 97, 119–20,
    122–23, 137–38, 142, 154, 156–
    57, 171–76
  views on slavery, 1–2, 6, 41, 46–48,
    124, 163
Brown's family:
  Dianthe (nee Lusk), 2, 172, 174
  Frederick, 5, 8, 10, 30, 172–74
  Jason, 8–10, 28–30, 38, 52

Brown's family (cont.):
  John, Jr., 2, 8, 10, 28–29, 31, 38–
    40, 59–61, 172, 174
  Mary (nee Day), 2–4, 9, 38, 87–89,
    91–92, 99, 100–102, 169
  Oliver, 16, 89
  Owen, 8, 16, 26, 29, 42
  Ruth, 8, 90
  Salmon, 8, 38
  Watson, 16, 89
Brown's raiding party:
  Anderson, Jeremiah, 153
  Anderson, Osborn, 43, 165–66
  Cook, John, 41, 43–46, 61–62, 146,
    152
  Copeland, John, 62, 166, 169–70
  Coppoc, Barclay, 62
  Coppoc, Edwin, 61
  Green, Shields, 56–57, 62, 164, 166,
    169
  Kagi, John, 14, 42–45, 53–56, 59–
    61, 146, 152
  Leary, Lewis, 62, 166
  Leeman, William, 45
  Merriam, Francis, 62
  Newby, Dangerfield, 166, 169
  Realf, Richard, 44–45, 150
  Stevens, A. D., 62, 68, 73–74, 146,
    152
  Thompson, Dauphin, 89
  Thompson, William, 89
  Tidd, Charles, 152
Buchanan, James, 36

C

Chase, Salmon P., 155
Chatham convention, 14, 33, 41–45,
  165

182